Books in the IGS Book Series
New Non-Aristotelian Library

Korzybski, Alfred (2010). *Selections from Science and Sanity.* (2nd Ed.). Edited by Lance Strate, with a Foreword by Bruce I. Kodish. Fort Worth, TX: Institute of General Semantics.

Strate, Lance (2011). *On the Binding Biases of Time and Other Essays on General Semantics and Media Ecology.* Fort Worth, TX: Institute of General Semantics.

Anton, Corey (2011). *Communication Uncovered: General Semantics and Media Ecology.* Fort Worth, TX: Institute of General Semantics.

Levinson, Martin H. (2012). *More Sensible Thinking.* New York, NY: Institute of General Semantics.

Anton, Corey & Strate, Lance (2012). *Korzybski and...* (Eds.) New York, NY: Institute of General Semantics.

Levinson, Martin H. (2014). *Continuing Education Teaching Guide to General Semantics.* New York, NY: Institute of General Semantics.

Berger, Eva & Berger, Isaac (2014). *The Communication Panacea: Pediatrics and General Semantics.* New York, NY: Institute of General Semantics.

Pace, Wayne R. (2017). *How to Avoid Making A Damn Fool of Yourself: An Introduction to General Semantics.* New York, NY: Institute of General Semantics.

Lahman, Mary P. (2018). *Awareness and Action: A Travel Companion.* New York, NY: Institute of General Semantics.

Levinson, Martin H. (2018). *Practical Fairy Tales For Everyday Living, Revised Second Edition.* New York, NY: Institute of General Semantics.

Levinson, Martin H. (2020). *Sensible Thinking for Turbulent Times: Revised Second Edition.* New York, NY: Institute of General Semantics.

Mayer, Christopher (2021). *How Do You Know?: A Guide to Clear Thinking About Wall Street, Investing, and Life.* New York, NY: Institute of General Semantics.

Levinson, Martin H. (2021). *Practical Fairy Tales For Everyday Living, Revised Second Edition*. New York, NY: Institute of General Semantics. (In Spanish)

Levinson, Martin H. (2021). *Practical Fairy Tales For Everyday Living, Revised Second Edition*. New York, NY: Institute of General Semantics. (In Hebrew)

Mayer, Christopher (2022). *Dear Fellow Time-Binder: Letters on General Semantics*. New York, NY: Institute of General Semantics.

Liñán, Laura Trujillo. (2022). *Formal Cause in Marshall McLuhan's Thinking*. New York, NY: Institute of General Semantics.

Strate, Lance (2022). *Concerning Communication: Epic Quests and Lyric Excursions Within the Human Lifeworld*. New York, NY: Institute of General Semantics.

Korzybski, Alfred (2023). *Science and Sanity: An Introduction to Non-Aristotelian Systems and General Semantics* (6th Ed.) New Preface by Lance Strate, New York, NY: Institute of General Semantics.

Korzybski, Alfred. (2024). *General Semantics Seminar 1937: Olivet College Lectures*. (4th Ed.) New York: Institute of General Semantics.

Strate, Lance. (2024). *Not A, Not Be, &C*. New York: Institute of General Semantics.

SENSIBLE THINKING 3

THE ADVENTURE CONTINUES

By
Martin H. Levinson

INSTITUTE OF GENERAL SEMANTICS

New Non-Aristotelian Library
INSTITUTE OF GENERAL SEMANTICS
New York, New York, USA

Published by the Institute of General Semantics
401 Park Avenue South #873
New York, NY, 10016
www.generalsemantics.org

Cover & Interior Book Design by Scribe Freelance
www.scribefreelance.com

ISBN: 978-1-970164-31-2 (Print)
978-1-970164-32-9 (eBook)
Published in the United States of America

Library of Congress Cataloging-in-Publication Data

Names: Levinson, Martin H., 1946- author.
Title: Sensible thinking 3 : the adventure continues / by Martin H. Levinson.
Other titles: Sensible thinking three
Description: New York : Institute of General Semantics, 2024. | Includes
    bibliographical references and index. | Summary: "Sensible Thinking 3 aims to
    help people think and communicate more effectively using the formulations
    of general semantics. Topics in it include practical ways to improve one's
    thinking ability, emotional self-management, understanding of the media, and
    analyses of social issues"– Provided by publisher.
Identifiers: LCCN 2024035361 (print) | LCCN 2024035362 (ebook) | ISBN
    9781970164312 (trade paperback) | ISBN 9781970164329 (ebook)
Subjects: LCSH: Thought and thinking. | Semantics (Philosophy)
Classification: LCC BF441. L483 2024 (print) | LCC BF441 (ebook) | DDC
    149/.94–dc23/eng/20241024
LC record available at https://lccn.loc.gov/2024035361
LC ebook record available at https://lccn.loc.gov/2024035362

To Steven Alter: mentor and friend

*Most people would rather die than think—
and that is what they do.*

—Bertrand Russell

Contents

Acknowledgments

Thank you: to Lance Strate, the President of the Institute of General Semantics, and the trustees of the Institute for your diligent efforts in promoting and preserving Alfred Korzybski's general system of evaluation; to Thom Gencarelli, the editor of *ETC: A Review of General Semantics*, for your excellent stewardship in keeping *ETC* one of the premiere academic journals around; to Corey Anton, the Vice President of the Institute of General Semantics and the head of the IGS Publications Committee, for your help in shepherding this book from manuscript to finished product; to Neil Postman, my doctoral dissertation advisor at NYU and ardent supporter of GS, for helping me to widen my appreciation and understanding of general semantics; to Harry Maynard, whose course in how to improve your thinking and communicating ability at Cooper Union introduced me to the field of general semantics; to Donna Lee McGullam, for her excellent editing work on the manuscript; to Daniel Middleton, the owner of Scribe Freelance, for his excellent work on the cover and interior design of the book; and to Katherine Liepe-Levinson, my wife and fellow writer, whose consistent support, advice, and encouragement sustained me in the completion of this project.

In addition, I need to thank the Institute of General Semantics, which has given me permission to reprint in a slightly different form the following pieces that have been published in *ETC: A Review of General Semantics*: "Why 'General' Semantics,"

ETC 70, no. 1 (January 2013): 22-24; "World War I: The Closing Period of the Childhood of Humanity," *ETC* 72, no. 2 (April 2015)149-156; "General Semantics and PTSD in the Military," *ETC* 72, no. 3 (July 2015): 258-264; "General Semantics and Constructive Political Discourse," *ETC* 80, no. 4 (October 2023): 495-502; "Dating Antisemitism: A Case Study," *ETC* 80, no. 3 (July 2023): 352-358; "Dating American Disunity," *ETC* 78, no. 1/2 (January and April 2021): 104-113; "Dating America's Response to Alcohol: An Historical Overview," *ETC* 80, no. 3 (July 2023): 385-393; "Dating Western Poetry," *ETC* 78, no. 1/2 (January and April 2021): 114-124; "Mapping the Language and Rhetoric of the Vietnam War," *ETC* 76, no. 3/4 (July/October 2019): 261-264; "What the Fuck: Examining an 'Obscene' Term," *ETC* 80, no. 1 (January 2023): 105-110; "A Brief History of the Institute of General Semantics on its Diamond Jubilee," *ETC* 70, no. 1 (January 2013): 5-12; "Indexing the American Revolutionary War" *ETC* no. 2 (April 2024): 185-192.

Introduction

Sensible Thinking 3: The Adventure Continues, like its forebears *Sensible Thinking for Turbulent Times* and *More Sensible Thinking,* aims to improve its readers' thinking abilities, emotional self-management, and analysis of social issues through the formulations of general semantics, a practical discipline that since 1933 when it was first introduced to the public can help one understand and better manage a world in flux.

General Semantics: An Effective Problem-Solving Approach

In the early part of the twentieth century, Alfred Korzybski, a trained engineer and a keen observer of the human condition, noted that scientists have great success solving technological problems and uncovering the mysteries of nature, while the nonscientific community has a poor record dealing with psychological and social issues. To improve the situation, Korzybski developed a science-oriented "self-help" system to assist individuals and groups to make more intelligent decisions in all aspects of their lives. He called this system *general semantics.*

A wide variety of writers, educators, therapists, and other professionals have drawn on and added to his system. Notable contributors include Steve Allen, polymath and writer of numerous books, including *Dumbth: 81 Ways to Make Americans Smarter* (idea number 81 is to learn general semantics); Alvin Toffler, author of *Future Shock*; Albert Ellis, originator of Rational Emotive Behavior Therapy; former US Senator S. I. Hayakawa, a student of Korzybski; and Neil Postman, founder of the media ecology program at NYU.

Many books have been published using general semantics to analyze and solve problems in areas such as education, communication, negotiation, management, social science, journalism, and personal adjustment. In addition, numerous articles on the benefits of general semantics have appeared in the *General Semantics Bulletin* and *ETC: A Review of General Semantics*, and more than 150 doctoral- and master's-degree studies have demonstrated its worth. General semantics is clearly a highly pragmatic discipline with a proven record of analyzing situations and solving problems.

Who Should Read *Sensible Thinking 3*?

Sensible Thinking 3 will appeal to general readers interested in improving their problem-solving abilities, as well as to college students, therapists, educators, employers, employees, politicians, leaders, thinkers, and others. It offers practical ways to gather information more accurately, evaluate it more clearly, and act upon it more successfully. While the book can be profitably perused in its entirety, each of the chapters can also stand alone. This means every chapter can be understood without the need to read preceding chapters.

Outline of The Book

Chapter Summaries

Part I—GS Theory and Applications

Chapter 1 offers a rationale for why general semantics is a useful discipline to study and employ.

Chapter 2 explores how general semantics can reduce cognitive distortions and improve the way we think and talk.

Chapter 3 provides clues to the early roots of general semantics.

Chapter 4 demonstrates how the use of GS formulations can mitigate the effects of post-traumatic stress disorder.

Part II—GS and Social Concerns

Chapter 5 supplies evidence on the beneficial effects of GS in promoting civil political conversations.

Chapter 6 discusses how GS can help change prejudicial modes of thinking.

Chapter 7 considers how GS can lead to a clearer understanding of the American legal system.

Part III—Dating Change Over Time

Chapter 8 shows via a GS device known as *dating* that political discord has been a feature not a bug in the long history of the United States.

Chapter 9 uses dating to investigate how America has responded to alcohol from the earliest days of the republic to the present.

Chapter 10 makes use of *dating* to illustrate how poetry has morphed through the centuries.

Part IV—The Map is Not the Territory

Chapter 11 discusses how labeling people and events affected the course of the Vietnam War.

Chapter 12 looks at the ways a familiar X-rated word has been employed by different people for different purposes in different eras.

Chapter 13 employs a GS thinking tool to analyze complexities often overlooked in studying the American Revolution.

Part V—Three GS Satires

Part V features 3 satires that are based on GS formulations.

Part VI—Three GS Poems

Part VI zooms in on 3 poems that relate to GS concerns.

Coda

A Brief History of the Institute of General Semantics chronicles the history of the Institute of General Semantics from the Institute's founding in 1938 to the present time.

PART I

GS Theory and Applications

Why "General" Semantics

General semantics (GS) does *not* mean the study of words. It largely involves applying the techniques, habits, and viewpoints of science to problems of everyday living. For example, rather than complaining about things that annoy you, GS encourages the use of the scientific method (observe, hypothesize, experiment, conclude) to change or cope with them.

GS was devised by Alfred Korzybski, a Polish-American-philosopher-scientist who proposed in the early part of the twentieth century that we replace the doctrine of survival of the fittest with the broader policy of the survival of humanity. To that end he postulated his celebrated "time-binding" theory, which features the idea that human beings are the only species that can pass symbolic information across generations. Animals cannot transfer such knowledge, which is why beavers still build their dams the same way their forerunners did thousands of years ago. Humans are able to live in skyscrapers rather than caves because of our ability to time-bind.

Korzybski observed that people have been crippling themselves for thousands of years through archaic Aristotelian reasoning inherited from the Greek philosopher Aristotle, who lived in the fourth century BCE

Three of Aristotle's assumptions in particular have led to poor ways of thinking: The Law of Identity (e.g., facts are facts, a stone is a stone, the truth is the truth), The Law of the Excluded Middle (something is either one thing or another—e.g., good or bad, tall or short, fat or thin), and The Law of Non-Contradiction (e.g., a fact is a fact and nothing but a fact). While you can argue that these laws are "common sense," GS reminds us that facts can change: (e.g., it was once considered a fact that the world was flat), things are rarely one thing or another (e.g., shades of gray not simply black or white), and something can be a fact and not a fact (e.g., The paradox: A barber shaves every man in the village who doesn't shave himself, who shaves the barber? Answer: To every rule there is an exception).

Individuals relate to their world the way they symbolize it, a notion that led Korzybski to "semantics," a word derived from the Greek *semantikos,* which means "to signify" or "stand for." Most people think of semantics as having to do *only* with the meaning and derivation of words. General semantics is interested in the meaning of *all* symbolic expressions—words, pictures, music, gestures, numbers, etc.—and what they mean to the person using and interpreting them.

To help people think more like scientists do, when they are engaging in the practice of science and trying to figure out what is going on in the world, GS recommends *operationalizing* vague expressions with concrete definitions. To wit, "happiness," "wealth," "success," and "failure" are somewhat fuzzy words without specific referents. Operationalizing them supplies such referents: Happiness, *to me,* is a warm cream cheese and jelly bagel. *I believe* wealth is having over a million dollars. *I think* success is getting an "A" in the course you are taking, "failure" is getting an "F." (GS notes that success and failure do not exist in nature. They are human constructions created by human beings for human purposes. It took Edison 10,000 tries to come up with a working light bulb. He said with each of those tries he successfully found another technique not to make a functioning bulb.)

Another way to be more scientific is to use what GS labels *extensional devices*. Such devices include:

- *Indexing*: Instead of simply "chair," think of chair$_1$, chair$_2$, chair$_3$, etc., noting differences among the chairs, as well as similarities. Indexing is a useful tool for combating stereotypical or prejudicial judgments (person$_1$, is not person$_2$, is not person$_3$, etc.). Indexing people, things, and events can be helpful in finding differences that might make a difference.

- *Dating*: America(2014) is not America(2024), you(today) are not you(last year), the Earth (in the third millennium) is not the Earth(ten thousand years ago). Dating reminds us that all things are constantly changing and that the world is in flux. As Heraclitus said, "You can't step in the same river twice."

- *Hyphenation*: Adding hyphens to "thing-events" (e.g., mind-body, space-time, matter-energy) that are normally split through language, but not separate in the "natural world," can assist us in grasping the complexity of the physical world.

- *Etc.*: Silently thinking "etcetera" when we experience or reflect on something can remind us that there is more in the world that can be taken in. You can't know all about anything; more can always be learned. Whatever you say it is, it isn't; there are always things you can add to your descriptions.

Let's take a closer look at "is." When we say, "The rose *is* red," "I *am* tall," "He *is* lazy," we are suggesting that redness is found in the rose, that tallness is found in me, and that laziness is found in him. When we use words in this manner we may act as if what we project outside ourselves can *actually be found* outside ourselves.

Bill Clinton, who probably never heard of general semantics, spoke like a general semanticist (and a lawyer) when he said, "It all depends on what the meaning of 'is' is."

Korzybski said that words are not the things they represent, or, as he more famously asserted, "the map is not the territory." Using this analogy, he suggested checking the map (words) against the territory ("reality") or against lower-order abstractions whenever possible. He advised that a good map has a structure similar to the territory (it has prediction value), that even the best maps become outdated sooner or later, and that different maps show different features of the same territory.

Imagine someone calls you an "idiot." You respond to the affront with a rise in blood pressure and a rapid rejoinder consisting of the words "Go to hell, you moron." Korzybski labeled quick reactions like these "signal reactions," and warned they are often injurious to the reactor. To modify such fast reactions he proposed delaying one's mental responses to stimuli since deferring such responses can allow one to engage the quarter inch of cerebral cortex with which we do our thinking. Benefits from delaying immediate reactions to insults, and other noxious verbal stimuli, can include not losing your friends, keeping your job, preserving your marriage, and avoiding physical harm from an angry antagonist whose signal response is to hit you.

Over the years, numerous individuals have employed general semantics to analyze and solve problems in a wide variety of fields including those of education, communication, negotiation, management, social science, journalism, and personal adjustment. In addition, numerous articles on the benefits of general semantics have appeared in the *General Semantics Bulletin* and *ETC: A Review of General Semantics* and more than 150 doctoral- and master's degree theses have demonstrated its efficacy. General semantics is a methodology with a wide range of applicability in diverse areas of human endeavor.

GS Techniques for Clear Thinking

Clear thinking is a type of human cognition that tends to make foresight as accurate as hindsight. With it we can more effectively solve problems of everyday living and spare ourselves needless suffering and time delays in coping with challenging situations and getting to our goals. Sadly, there can be blocks to clear thinking in the form of cognitive biases—systematic errors in thinking that affect the decisions and judgments we make. This chapter shows how general semantics can help to mitigate ten of those biases.[1]

Ten Cognitive Biases with General Semantics Correctives

1. Confirmation Bias

> "What the human being is best at doing is interpreting all new information so that their prior conclusions remain intact."
>
> —Warren Buffett

Confirmation bias is the tendency to interpret new information so that it becomes compatible with our existing theories, beliefs, and convictions. It involves sifting out any new information that may test such theories, beliefs, and convictions. By not seeking out objective facts, interpreting information in ways that only props up one's existing beliefs, and only recalling details that affirm a person's convictions, confirmation bias leads people to often miss vital information.

Examples of confirmation bias include the following:

- During election season people tend to seek information that puts their favorite candidates in a good light. They will also look for evidence that that discredits candidates they oppose.
- Investors frequently rely more heavily on information that confirms their pre-existing beliefs regarding the value of certain stocks.
- There are doctors who search for new information selectively to verify their preliminary diagnosis.

To guard against confirmation bias (a term that did not exist in the nineteenth century), Charles Darwin wrote down and thought about arguments and observations that went contra to his theory. Darwin understood the propensity in people to fail to see disconfirming evidence. The truer he judged his theory's accuracy, the more actively he searched for discrepancies.

The scientific method, a technique employed in general semantics to solve problems of everyday living, can be a useful tool to combat confirmation bias. That is because the scientific method is based on the principle that a proposition or theory cannot be scientific if it does not have the possibility of being shown false. People that employ the scientific method are open to the idea that what they are hypothesizing may not be accurate and that there is worth in considering new information and evidence.

Other useful approaches to battle confirmation bias include searching for information from a range of sources, viewing situations from varied perspectives, and discussing one's thoughts with others.

2. The Problems with Averages

"There are three kinds of lies: lies, damned lies, and statistics."

—Mark Twain

If the average net worth of a person in a town of a hundred people is $75,000 and Jeff Bezos moves into the community what happens to that average? Answer: It will rise sharply with the average net worth of individuals in that town now being in the millions.

It's commonly thought the divorce rate in the US is fifty percent. But when one looks at specific groupings such as age, level of educational attainment, profession, race, geography, religious belief, etc. that number may vary by category or mix of categories.

How many hits does the average website get? There is no such thing as an average website. A minority of sites (e.g., Google, YouTube, Facebook, Instagram, Open AI) get the most hits, and countless others get relatively few.

How many copies does an average book sell? How much money does an average doctor earn? What is the average success of an ad campaign? What is the average daily fluctuation in the Dow Jones Index? Whatever the numbers show, unless you're familiar with the term "power law"—a statistical notion whereby a few extremes dominate the distribution—the concept of average is not very useful.

Indexing, a GS tool that involves examining individual cases within larger categories, can help us to be wary of the pitfalls involved with "averaging." For example, person$_1$ whose net worth is 75,000 dollars is not person$_2$ whose new worth is two billion dollars; person$_1$ who marries before the age of 18 (people who marry before the age of 18 have a 48% likelihood of being divorced in 10 years) is not person$_2$ who marries after the age of 25 (people who marry after the age of 25 have a much lower likelihood of getting divorced than people who marry before the age of 18); and website$_1$ (which if it's Google receives tens of thousands of searches per second on any given day) is not website$_2$ (which if it's mine receives less than a thousand hits a year). Indexing shows there are no universals in the "real world." Each person or thing is unique and possesses unique characteristics.

3. Action Bias

"All of humanity's problems stem from man's inability to sit quietly in his room alone."

—Blaise Pascal

Action bias is a tendency to do something, even if one doesn't know what to do. For example, soccer goalies have almost no time to react to where the ball is going after a penalty kick. Most lunge right or left rather than stay at the center of the net to block a goal. They do this even though numerous studies show that goalkeepers standing at the center stop about a third of the shots. But the dives look good to the fans and feel less shameful than standing firm watching the ball whiz by, even though standing in place is a perfectly valid choice.

Other examples of action bias include the following: (a) newbie investors often buy stocks when they don't have the knowledge or experience to critique the market; (b) doctors who can't diagnose a patient's illness are more prone to prescribe a course of treatment rather than wait for more evidence; (c) rookie police officers sometimes worsen potentially violent situations by acting too soon rather than letting time pass to allow the situations to simmer down.

In the Stone Age, when humans were prey to creatures such as saber-toothed cats, predatory kangaroos, giant hyenas, and other wild beasts, an action bias made a certain sense, as running away from an iffy concern was better than the chance of winding up as an animal's dinner. But today's world favors reflective thinking, which makes cortex-motivated delayed reactions (responses Korzybski pointed to as a major factor that separates humans from the rest of the animal kingdom) essential to effective human functioning. Being conscious of the way we abstract and conditionally respond to stimuli is by and large far more useful in successfully navigating situations than reacting in a knee-jerk way.

4. Sunk Cost Fallacy

> "When the facts change, I change my mind. What do you do, sir?"
>
> —John Maynard Keynes

Sunk cost fallacy refers to the fallacy of privileging sunk costs, which rationally should be ignored. For example, Olivia buys a nonrefundable movie ticket to a film she begins watching and hates. Should Olivia keep watching the movie because she's paid for it and can't get her money back? If she does she has become victim to the sunk choice fallacy. The money she's laid out for her movie ticket is a sunk cost that should not affect her decision. Some people stay in romantic relationships longer than they should because of the sunk cost fallacy—they think if they exit the relationship they will have wasted all the time spent in it.

The sunk cost fallacy is occasionally referred to as the "Concorde fallacy," which has to do with the fact that the British and French governments continued funding the Concorde even though it was a consistent economic loser. One can argue America's escalation in the Vietnam War involved a sunk cost fallacy, as increased troop buildups were made because of losses sustained. Those losses were a sunk cost and should not have factored into the decision.

The general semantics notion of *dating* can diminish privileging sunk costs by reminding us that things change—the Vietnam War(1966) is not the Vietnam War(1969); the Concorde(when it was first envisioned) is not the Concorde(ten years later); money spent on a movie ticket(in anticipation of seeing a movie you think you will like) does not have the same value as money spent on a movie ticket(on a film you are watching and can't stand). While it sometimes makes sense to stay the course, often it's best to cut your losses. When that's the case one can seek comfort in these words of Ralph Waldo Emerson: "A foolish consistency is the hobgoblin of little minds."

5. The Overconfidence Effect

> "We see what we see because we miss all the finer details."
>
> —Alfred Korzybski

The overconfidence effect has to do with a person's subjective confidence in their judgments being reliably greater than the objective accuracy of those judgments, particularly when that confidence is very high. This bias is sometimes labeled the "Lake Wobegon" effect after Garrison Keillor's mythical Minnesota town where "all the women are strong, all the men are good-looking, and all the children are above average." The overconfidence effect occurs more with men, is exhibited by experts as much as or more than laypeople, and is often seen in optimists. Even pessimists overrate themselves, though to a lesser degree than those sporting rose-colored glasses.

Examples of the overconfidence effect include: (a) people who think they are much "smarter" than they truly are—those individuals could show their overconfidence by not studying for their exams and as a result getting lower scores than if they had studied for them; (b) political candidates who, confident they are going to win their elections, do not aggressively campaign and as a consequence of their overconfidence lose their elections and; (c) gamblers, who confident of their ability to predict the next flip of a card, lose their money because of their presumptuousness.

People who are overconfident are employing, in GS parlance, an *intensional orientation*—a tendency to view people, objects, and events in a highly subjective manner. A better approach to understanding "what is really going on" in situations would be to employ an *extensional orientation*—taking a hard look at the actual people, things, and events one is encountering and then forming conclusions. An extensional orientation is biased toward trying to see the world more as it "is" rather than the way one would like it to be.

6. Alternative Blindness

"You're either with us or against us in the fight against terror."

—President George W. Bush

The Greek philosopher Aristotle (384–322 BCE) was a careful observer of his culture and its language structure. From his observations, he derived what has come to be known as the "laws of thought," tools of logic very much with us today. One of those laws is "the law of the excluded middle"—a thing is either "A" or "not A." The law of the excluded middle encourages us to believe that every question can be answered in terms of "either-or."

The English language pushes us in either-or directions. Its many polarizing terms (e.g., good/bad, hot/cold, tall/short, thin/fat) lead us to think in extremes rather than through gradations.

Either-or thinking keeps us from noticing the great diversity in the world. For example, people do not come in two varieties: tall or short. If we lined up everyone in the United States and arranged them according to height, we would have at one end of the line professional basketball players and at the other end "little people." Between these two groups would be the vast majority of individuals.

Most things we encounter are more accurately mapped by a statistical distribution rather than through either-or terms. This idea can be seen on a bell curve of normal distribution. If you plot instances from daily life, such as days above and below 100°F, IQ, height, weight on a graph, it is the middle range that has the most distribution. Either-or comparisons show up at the two extreme ends of the graph.

To get past either-or thinking, general semantics recommends using a *multivalued approach*. This approach involves examining more than just two alternatives. Case in point: It is Friday evening, and you want to relax after a hard week. You think, "I'll either go to the movies or stay home and watch TV." Sadly, the movie- and TV programs that are on do not seem very appealing. So, what can you do? A student of general semantics would suggest employing a multivalued approach, which would allow you to brainstorm additional possibilities—attend a play, read a book, go out to dinner, walk around the neighborhood, etc. In life, there are rarely only two choices.

7. The Fallacy of the Single Cause

"It is indeed a common plague of humanity. . . . The fallacy of attributing to one cause what is due to many causes."

—Alfred Korzybski

We live in a process world. But our language does not accurately reflect this fact because it allows us to "split" with words what cannot be split in the world "out there." For example, we talk about the "mind" and "body" as if they were separate entities. But that is not correct. Can there be a mind without a body? Lacking a body, there would be no mind. And without the mind, what would the body be? Moreover, the chemical processes of the body affect the mind—that's why antidepressants work. And the opposite is true. Our mental state can influence our physical condition—worry can aggravate bodily ailments.

GS labels our tendency to use words in isolation as *elementalism*. We practice elementalism when we let the word "flower" make us forget that the "real" flower is an ever-changing process that entails air, light, water, and soil. When we use words to talk about a flower we should not fool ourselves into thinking we are fully describing a real flower.

Elementalism is involved when we seek the cause of something, unconsciously assuming there is only one cause—for example, the cause of juvenile delinquency, the reason for cancer, the root of unhappiness. Yet most problems in life do not have single antecedents. Causation is typically multifaceted.

Elementalism is firmly established in our language and when we use words its effects cannot totally be avoided. But there are GS tools that can mitigate its power. For instance, we can use hyphens to connect false-to-fact "elementalistic" terms to suggest those terns refer to inseparable nonverbal events. Einstein, recognizing the "one-ness" of space and time, created the notion of *space-time*. Other non-elementalistic terms include *psycho-biological*, *neuro-linguistic*, and *organism-as-a-whole-in-environments*.

We can also place quotes around words that suggest false-to-fact structures—for example, "thoughts" and "feelings." (Mental states and emotional states do not take place in isolation. Thoughts and feelings influence each other.)

And we can add a silent "etc." to our thinking—"mind, etc.," "thoughts, etc.," "feelings, etc." Adding etc. indicates there is always more that can be learned, more that can be said.

8. Neglect of Probability

"Life is a school of probability."

—Walter Bagehot

Neglect of probability is a cognitive bias based on the tendency to disregard probability when making decisions. It is one way in which people break the typical rules for decision-making. Small risks are either neglected or hugely overrated. The continuum between extremes is ignored.

An example of this bias can be seen in a situation where a person is as afraid of a 1% chance as of a 99% chance of contamination from germs. Another example involves people who fear flying, because they fear being killed in a plane crash—such individuals typically never think about the dangers of crossing a street, a behavior far more likely to result in death than flying. Terrorism is effective partly because of the neglect of probability, as people often don't consider the extremely remote possibility that they will be injured or die from an act of terrorism.

Consider the following hypothetical: Emily thinks it is a good idea to wear seatbelts in cars, as many studies show wearing seatbelts saves lives. Amelia takes the opposite view. She read about an accident where a car went into a river and the driver drowned because he could not release his seatbelt. In another accident, she says, a seatbelt prevented someone from escaping a car that was on fire.

In the above scenario, a sensible approach for deciding whether to wear a seatbelt would be to weigh the probabilities: thousands of studies showing seatbelts save lives versus two specific instances where seatbelts led to the reverse effect. Such statistical analysis would lead a rational person to conclude that to maximize your chances of surviving an accident one should buckle up.

Probability thinking plays an important role in most fields of scientific research and, when applied to the problems of everyday living, can help people to make good decisions. The trick is to do it, which isn't much of a trick given the probability that in most cases it will produce more efficient and effective outcomes than avoiding its application.

9. The News Illusion

"News is to the mind what sugar is to the body."

—Rolf Dobelli

Every day countless events take place throughout the world but only some are reported on and brought to the public's attention. Those events, if they are reported, become the news of the day. This was not always the case.

Prior to the invention of the telegraph in 1844, the news of the day consisted largely of the goings-on in one's local community. News reports could only be delivered as fast as a train could travel. The telegraph, which brought as great an information revolution in the nineteenth century as the internet has today, changed that. It delivered messages instantly and in so doing, as Neil Postman points out in his book *Amusing Ourselves to Death*, brought about an information environment filled with irrelevant information that has expanded exponentially in today's electronic world.

News shows on television are full of attention-grabbing stories, dramatic images, and sensational "facts" to capture our attention. The result is viewers who walk around with distorted "mental maps" of the risks and threats present in the world. As for relevancy, does a plane crash in Russia, the resignation of the president of Sierra Leone, or the goings-on of celebrity couples make any difference to the lives of most people?

One way to insulate ourselves from the hype and haphazardness of TV news programs would be to not watch them. If that's a bridge too far, some other ways to protect yourself from the hysteria and disjunction rife on TV news shows are the following: understand there is a reason it's called a "show," try to determine what in the broadcast is important, try to figure out (from the language being used) the connection between the commercials and the fears and motivations of American consumers, see if you can ascertain the assumptions behind questions being asked during the program.

10. The False Causality Fallacy

> "to measure cause and effect... you must ensure that a simple correlation, however tempting it may be, is not mistaken for a cause."
>
> —Neal deGrasse Tyson

The false causality fallacy is based on the mistaken assumption that because one event follows another, the first event caused the second. Some examples of the false causality fallacy are these:

- Researchers found that long periods in the hospital affected people adversely. Health insurers were pleased with that news. But the fact is, patients who are discharged quickly are very likely healthier than those who are kept for treatment.

- A study showed a strong positive correlation between ice cream consumption and homicide rates (ice cream consumption and crime tend to increase as the weather gets warmer through the spring and summer months). Does eating ice cream cause people to commit violent crimes? Of course not. Correlation does not necessarily equal causation.

- Liam eats corn flakes for breakfast each day. Once, he had eggs instead, and there was a massive earthquake in the city where he lived. He has eaten corn flakes ever since.

As mentioned earlier, correlation does not equal causation. It just shows a relationship between variables. Before going beyond that notion to "cause and effect," one would be wise to gather factual evidence demonstrating such a conclusion. To aid in such gathering one can apply the following distinctions made by Irving J. Lee, the author of *Language Habits in Human Affairs* and other GS books, between statements of facts and inferences.

Statements of fact
1. Made after observation or experience
2. Are confined to what one observes or experiences
3. Only a limited number can be made
4. Represents a high degree of probability, is close to certainty

Statements of inference
1. Made anytime—before, during, or after observation
2. Go beyond what one observes or experiences
3. Can make an unlimited number in any situation
4. Represent some degree of probability

Correlation and causation are not the same thing. Sometimes what is presented as the cause turns out to be the effect, and sometimes the reverse holds true. And sometimes there just is no connection—like with eggs and earthquakes.

Manhood of Humanity Revisited

Korzybski's Vision: A Manhood of Humanity

Reacting to the terrible slaughter of World War I, Alfred Korzybski felt impelled to offer a vision for a peaceful and more civilized world. In 1921, he presented that vision in *Manhood of Humanity: The Science and Art of Human Engineering*—Korzybski used "Manhood" in the accepted 1920s sense of humankind. The book explores how the energies and capacities of human beings can be channeled for the advancement of humanity. In 1950, shortly after Korzybski's death, a second edition of *Manhood of Humanity* was published, in which the subtitle was eliminated.

Korzybski believed the world had been greatly shaken by World War I and that its occurrence spelled the end of the "childhood of humanity," a state historically devoid of any real understanding of humanistic values. He noted, "From the early days of humanity, dogmatic theology, law, ethics, and science in its infancy, were the monopolies of one class and the source of their power. The first to break that power were the exact sciences. They progressed too rapidly to be bound by obscure old writings and prejudices; life and realities were their domain."[1]

Korzybski maintained in *Manhood of Humanity* that humanity's *manhood* will be a scientific period, "[A] period that will witness the gradual extension of scientific method to all the

36

interests of mankind—a period in which man will discover the essential nature of man and establish, at length, the science and art of directing human energies and human capacities to the advancement of human weal in accordance with the laws of human nature."[2] Korzybski considered technological progress a good thing. Its negative uses were due to human misevaluations. Those are what led to difficulties.

Korzybski declared a functional re-definition of man was necessary for human beings to understand their position in evolutionary development. Human beings, he argued, as opposed to plants and animals, are *time-binders* that have the capacity to improve on the accumulated abstractions of others and transmit those abstractions to the next generation. Beavers may be remarkable builders of dams, but they do not progress in the way of inventions or further development. People are not like beavers, who build their dams the same way from one generation to another. We begin where others have left off and set out to build better dams.

Korzybski argued that human values relating to power, status, lifestyle, etc. are largely based on systems and human interactions that involve subjugating the living by manipulating time-binding knowledge created by the dead. He advocated, instead, for cooperation in place of competition and self-improvement in place of selfishness, greed, territorialism, etc. Korzybski thought human beings are not set by nature but changeable through education and he devoted himself to discovering why we copy animals in our nervous reactions. That search culminated in 1933 with the publication of *Science and Sanity: An Introduction to Non-Aristotelian Systems and General Semantics*, which formally introduced general semantics to the world.

Korzybski was aware that it would not be easy for humanity to leave its childhood, which he noted had been "inconceivably long" and marked with relatively little progress. And, given all the violence and chaos taking place in the world these days, it seems our species still has a long way to go to reach "adult status." However, Korzybski thought the game worth the candle, which is evidenced by the following comment he made in the concluding chapter of *Manhood of Humanity*: "If only this little book will *initiate* the scientific study of Man, I shall be happy; for then we may confidently expect a science and art that will know how to direct the energies of man to the advancement of the human weal."[3]

The Impetus for *Manhood of Humanity*

"The conclusion of the World War is the closing of the period of the childhood of humanity."

—Alfred Korzybski, *Manhood of Humanity*

Shocked by the immense destruction that followed World War I, Alfred Korzybski, a twice-wounded veteran on the Eastern Front, attempted to answer the question of how human beings are able to make such effective technological progress yet make such a hash of human affairs.

The lack of headway in harmonious human interactions was evident to Korzybski by the occasion of World War I (*aka* the "Great War" and "A War to End All Wars"), a horrific and tragic event brought about by nationalism, narcissism, jealousy, greed, domestic concerns, and a host of other factors. It seemed to Korzybski that little had changed in the tendency of groups to fight one another. What had changed, he observed, was the advanced technology that created the destructive weapons used during WW1. Those weapons made the First World War significantly more terrible than the wars that preceded it. Ten million soldiers died in the conflict, twenty million were severely wounded, and eight million returned home permanently disabled.

H.G. Wells (a prolific English writer, best now remembered for his science fiction novels), like Korzybski, was appalled by "man's increasing power of destruction" during the Great War. He made this position clear in an article he published in 1915 in the *New York Times* titled "Civilization at the Breaking Point."[4] In that piece, Wells showed he understood that technology had altered the face of combat in World War I and had brought with it killing on a scale unimaginable before that struggle. This technology, the awful fruits of which led Korzybski to publish *Manhood of Humanity* and twelve years later *Science and Sanity*, epitomized to Korzybski the childhood of humanity, a childhood symbolized by the use of updated, powerful, destructive weaponry. Some of that weaponry, which unloosed death and destruction the likes of which the world had never seen before, is described in the following section.

Some of the Deadly Weapons of World War I

Machine Guns

Arguably, the most noteworthy technological enhancement during World War I was the improvement of the machine gun, a weapon originally developed by Hiram Maxim, an American-born inventor. The Germans recognized its military potential and had large numbers of machine guns ready to use when the war began in 1914. The British and French quickly caught up to the Germans and produced thousands of these automatic arms that could fire 450-600 rounds a minute. Men who went over-the-top in trenches swiftly became casualties when the enemy opened fire with machine guns. The machine gun, along with barbed wire and mines, transformed what could have been a war of rapid advance and conquest into an endless struggle of defense.

Tanks

The Allies built the first tanks in 1915 and 1916, but their use did not become widespread until 1917. Tank development was a response to the deadlock trench warfare had created on the Western Front. Though highly unreliable, tanks brought a measure of mobility to the battlefield. The Germans were slow to develop tanks in World War I but they took note of them, and by World War II they were producing some of the most formidable tanks in the world.

Poison Gas

Poison gas was probably the most feared of all WW I weapons. It could be used on the trenches even when no attack was going on. Chlorine gas was employed for the first time on a large scale at the Second Battle of Ypres in April 1915. German soldiers used it against the Allied forces. The British expressed outrage at Germany's use of poison gas but responded by creating their own gas warfare capability. Many who survived gas attacks went blind or suffered severe lung damage. The horrors of World War I gas attacks led many countries to sign in 1925 a protocol to the Third Geneva Convention banning the use, but not the production, of biological and chemical weapons in war.

Artillery

The most intensively and extensively used weapon in World War I was artillery, the shells of which killed or maimed more men in the trenches than any other armament. During World War I artillery became larger, easier to handle, and more accurate. At the Battle of the Somme in 1916, almost 1.8 million artillery rounds were fired on German lines in the space of a week. The largest single artillery piece was the German-built "Paris Gun," which was used to pummel the French capital from 75 miles away. World

War I was the first armed struggle in history in which the cannons used did not have to be re-aimed after every shot, due to the recoil-absorbing mechanisms built into the cannons.

Submarines

The first "modern" submarines were designed in the United States in the 1880s. By the start of World War I, submarine technology had greatly improved. Submarines could go deeper, to about 150 feet, and had guns mounted on deck. To protect ships against submarine attacks, the Royal Navy introduced the convoy system, which made use of aircraft for escorts, especially in coastal waters. During World War I, the convoy system led to sharp declines in the scale of German submarine damage, which totaled more than twelve million tons (over 5,000 ships) by the war's end.

Flamethrowers

The earliest flamethrowers dated back to the 5th century BCE. In subsequent centuries they were refined. During WW1 the Germans made effective use of the portable *flammenwerfer* (flamethrower), with gas cylinders strapped to the backs of soldiers using it. The British came out with the *Livens Large Gallery Flame Projector*, a weapon 56 feet long and 5,000 pounds in weight that took a carrying party of 300 men to convey it to the front line to assemble. The French devised the portable one-man *Schilt* flamethrower, which was used in trench attacks during 1917-18. Flamethrowers were incendiary devices designed to kill and disfigure and, perhaps more importantly, dishearten the enemy.

Rifles

Soldiers in World War I were equipped with bolt-action rifles that provided mechanical reloading capabilities from spring-loaded clips inserted into rifle magazines. Cartridges were not hand rolled, as was so in earlier times—munitions factories produced a composite of bullet, propellant, and primer. Rifles could kill a man at a distance of 1500 yards and because they were so effective they made advancements and offensives difficult. Snipers used their rifles to target moving objects behind enemy lines. Though the overall number of casualties claimed by snipers was small, they played a significant role in sapping enemy morale.

Grenades

The grenade proved an ideal weapon for stopping large groups of charging foes or clearing trenches packed with enemies. The first "safe" grenade was the *Mills Bomb*, invented by Englishman, William Mills in 1915—until then, grenades had often proved as deadly to the thrower as to the intended target. The Germans developed numerous grenade models including the *stielhandgranate* (stick bomb), the *diskushandgranate* (disc grenade), and the *kugelhandgranate* (ball grenade). The German army also employed gas grenades.

Airplanes

In addition to using airplanes for reconnaissance, both sides engaged in aerial bombing. Fighter pilots who downed five or more enemy aircraft were labeled aces and portrayed as modern knights. Most pilots in planes that were downed died, as aviators were not allowed to wear parachutes. Planes became more deadly with the invention of the "interrupter gear," a timing mechanism that synchronized the machine gun with the moving propeller blades. The First World War encouraged the rapid upgrade of the airplane as a combat weapon, which in ensuing years would be yet another instrument of instant, high-tech, anonymous destruction.

Martin H. Levinson

One Hundred Years Later

Since the publication of *Manhood of Humanity* in 1921, the world has suffered through World War II, the Holocaust, the dropping of atomic bombs on cities, a Cold War that led to stand-in hot wars, and an ongoing "War on Terror." Climate change has become much worse and the world has experienced a pandemic triggered by human negligence and abetted by a disregard for science by hundreds of millions of people who refused to get vaccinated to prevent and lessen the effects of Covid-19.

On the plus side, nine nations currently possess nuclear weapons but such devices have not been used since 1945 and little atomic testing is presently going on. Climate-change mitigation strategies may have helped slow rising temperatures and the demise of Planet Earth. And there is hope that as unvaccinated people become more health-literate, more people will agree to be vaccinated to protect themselves and others from Covid.

On the to-be-determined side, the advent of television, the internet, and social media has made the sharing of information, and misinformation, instantaneous. These technologies have become useful tools of division for those who seek to manipulate people for political and economic advantage. Whether that process can be slowed down or reversed is unclear.

On the things-are-already-decided side, some people feel, unlike the boundless sense of optimism in the inevitability of progress widespread in the 1920s, that progress is not inevitable, or even desirable. Rather than looking forward to a better future for themselves and those they care about, these individuals see the world as a dark and threatening place and those inhabiting it as not bright or attentive enough to save themselves and humanity from extinction. Contra Korzybski, who had great faith in science, the scientific method, and education to move our species forward, they believe the game is over for human advancement.

What would Korzybski say to such individuals, and others who seem more interested in being loyal to members of a tribe than being loyal to the idea of human development? It's hard to know, but perhaps the author of *Manhood of Humanity* might respond with a quote from that book, telling these partisans "We cannot be psychological isolationists and try to be constructive time-binders, or we are bound to be bogged down in a social morass of conflicts. . . . We must begin to realize our potentialities as humans, then we may approach the future with some hope. . . . The evolution of human development may be retarded, but (in the end) it cannot be stopped."[5]

4

General Semantics and PTSD

Combat-related posttraumatic stress disorder (PTSD) is a long-standing problem dating back to antiquity. Homer's epic poems the *Iliad* and the *Odyssey* are filled with descriptions of war-related psychological damage. Throughout the Middle Ages, religious rituals of penance were used to resolve inner suffering emanating from combat.

In American history, each successive war the nation has fought in has led to new names for what we now label PTSD and new theories about its causes. In the post-Civil War era, two models attempted to explain combat-related trauma sustained by soldiers who fought in the Civil War. On the physiological side, doctors called such trauma "Soldier's Heart" or "Da Costa's Syndrome" (named after Joseph Mendes Da Costa, who investigated and described the condition during the Civil War), as many soldiers reacted to the strain of the Civil War with cardiac disorders. On the psychological side, soldiers were also labeled as suffering from "nostalgia"—the idea being that soldiers who fought on alien terrain developed symptoms because they yearned to be back home.

In WWI, it was called *shell shock*—a response to artillery fire and warfare that resulted in feelings of powerlessness that could manifest as fear, panic, flight, or incapacity to reason, sleep, walk, or talk. Charles Myers, a Cambridge psychologist, was the first to use the phrase "shell shock" in an article he published in *The Lancet* in 1915.[1] Though no longer employed in medical or military discourse, the label "shell shock," an alliterative and rather catchy expression, gained credence with the public as an emblematic injury of WWI.

During WWII, doctors dubbed combat-related trauma as *battle fatigue, combat neurosis,* and *combat exhaustion.* Some generals, most notably George S. Patton Jr., who is said to have slapped two soldiers recuperating from posttraumatic stress in a military hospital and referred to one as a "yellow bastard" who should not be admitted to the hospital, made the untrue assumption that combat-related trauma was based on weakness and cowardice— generals throughout history have believed this false inference. The Army refuted this notion when, reflecting a consensus that all soldiers were vulnerable to battle fatigue, in 1944 it adopted the slogan, "Every man has his breaking point."

During the Korean War, mental health professionals used the expression *gross stress reaction,* a term contained in the 1952 edition of the *Diagnostic and Statistical Manual* (DSM-I), published by the American Psychiatric Association. That locution was included in the *DSM* as a response to the psychological damage that mental health providers had seen in soldiers who had fought during WWII. The term "gross stress reaction" was not included in the *DSM-II,* which was published in 1968.

After the Vietnam War, in 1980, the medical world acknowledged *PTSD* as a legitimate medical disorder by listing it in the *DSM-III.* Today, largely due to the efforts of Vietnam veterans (and other veterans that have served in subsequent conflicts) who fought to have the disorder taken seriously, PTSD is considered a recognized medical ailment characterized by four core indicators: intrusion symptoms, avoidance, hyperarousal, and negative alterations in cognition and mood that require treatment. In 2012, the federal government spent three billion dollars on

PTSD treatment for veterans, a figure that does not include billions in PTSD disability payments made every year to former service members.²

General Semantics as a Treatment for Posttraumatic Stress

Douglas Kelley, an army psychiatrist and student of general semantics (GS) founder Alfred Korzybski, along with medical professionals that he trained, used GS to treat over 7,000 soldiers for symptoms of posttraumatic stress between 1943 and 1945 at the 312th Station Hospital near Staffordshire, England, and the 130th General Hospital in Ciney, Belgium.³ Kelley, the chief consultant in Clinical Psychology and assistant consultant in Psychiatry to the European Theater of Operations (and the chief psychiatrist in charge of the prisoners at Nuremberg), described how GS was used to treat military posttraumatic stress in an article he published in 1951 in *The Journal of Nervous and Mental Diseases* titled "The Use of General Semantics and Korzybskian Principles as an Extensional Method of Group Psychotherapy in Traumatic Neuroses."⁴

The protocol Kelley and his colleagues used with soldiers under treatment was to conduct five group lecture/discussion sessions, each lasting an hour, which showed how GS could improve psychological functioning. Sessions could go over the hour if the participants wanted them to. They often did.

The first half hour of each meeting involved (a) providing the counselees an explanation of posttraumatic stress symptoms, (b) a justification of the treatment employed, and (c) a discussion on overcoming symptoms already present and ways to prevent symptoms that might develop in the future. During these 30 minutes, formal presentations of GS ideas and formulations were kept to a minimum, as it was thought supplying lots of material in this part of the discussion would lead patients to think the therapist was simply lecturing them. GS ideas and formulations were talked about at greater length during the informal discussion period scheduled for the second half hour.

Kelley believed anyone with sufficient maturity could be taught to run the GS groups, and to help nonpsychiatric workers do that he gave them mimeographed information on general semantics. He reported this strategy worked out very well.[5] He also reported that medical officers of the 29th Infantry Division were given comprehensive training in GS ideas and formulations and that the 29th Division had a relatively low incidence of neuropsychiatric disorders during the early days of the Normandy invasion.[6]

Kelley noted the efficacy of using GS to treat posttraumatic stress was demonstrated by the high recovery rates in the European Theater from hospitals where GS methods were employed.[7] He also noted GS helped to prevent recurrent posttraumatic stress: "Here Korzybski's extensional method of dating and indexing is most important. His other techniques are, of course, of value but these two simple devices proved remarkably potent in this type of neurotic reaction."[8]

Captain James A. Saunders, an enthusiastic student of *Science and Sanity* who had worked as a liaison officer on the Senate Committee on Naval Affairs, described and evaluated Kelley's approach in a 1946 memorandum written to the Chief of Naval Personnel:

> By means of pictures, charts and lectures the men [receiving treatment for combat exhaustion] were instructed in the structure of the human nervous system, the manner in which it functioned and the relationship between events in the external world and the human nervous system. He [Kelley] taught them physico-mathematical methods of evaluation, including

the use of the extensional techniques of thinking. The men who were able to understand and use the new methods of evaluation were able to reevaluate their combat experiences and overcome their psychoneuroses. They were also able to use the new methods of evaluation and make appropriate adjustments to the new experiences they encountered in combat in the European Theatre of Operations.[9]

Alfred Korzybski understood posttraumatic stress firsthand, as he had suffered its effects as a combat veteran of WWI. Two symptoms that troubled him in civilian life were insomnia and thoughts he would be bombed when airplanes flew above him. Using GS notions, Korzybski freed himself from these and other posttraumatic stress reactions. He said in dealing with posttraumatic stress it is important to work on minimizing second order reactions, such as fear of fear, nervousness about nervousness, worry about worry, etc., as such reactions can seriously aggravate one's responses to posttraumatic stress.[10]

A WWII Veteran's Readjustment and Extensional Methods

Korzybski recounted some of his experiences with posttraumatic stress in an article titled "A Veteran's Re-Adjustment and Extensional Methods," which was published in *ETC: A Review of General Semantics* shortly after WWII.[11] The article included a case report titled "A Veteran Uses General Semantics for Rehabilitation" that described the experience of a WWII veteran who used GS to treat himself for symptoms of posttraumatic stress. The veteran had learned GS ideas and formulations as a student in a 10-hour GS course taught by Professor Elwood Murray at the University College (evening division) of the University of Denver.

The veteran had been discharged from the army for "nervous disability" and was suffering from several debilitating posttraumatic stress symptoms when he was introduced to GS methodology, which he constructively put into practice to overcome his condition. For example, he employed GS to help him conquer his fear of darkness and fear of crowds. He specifically used the GS notion of delayed evaluation to tamp down feelings of immediate anger in conversations, feeling nervous when watching war movies, and assuming movements in trees and bushes were those of enemy combatants.[12]

To modify his misconception of police, fire, and ambulance sirens as signaling air raids—which caused him to break into a sweat and want to drop to the ground—the veteran adopted a GS extensional approach and visited a fire station where he inspected the sirens on the trucks. This helped him to rationally evaluate siren sounds and not panic when he heard them. He also visited an airfield and examined the planes there, which helped him understand the dissimilarity between aircraft(1943) flying over Japanese-held islands with malicious intent and aircraft(1945) flying in the United States transporting passengers.

Utilizing the scientific method (observe, hypothesize, experiment, and conclude), the veteran was able to reduce his reflexive negative identifications by exposing himself to the conditions that caused such identifications. For example, when he first returned home he developed a huge dislike of dogs, an antipathy caused by his experience with dogs he encountered overseas. He had seen those dogs devouring the bodies of American and Japanese soldiers, which was, naturally, quite repulsive to him.

When he came back to the United States, the veteran experienced feelings of revulsion whenever he came upon a dog. To resist having such feelings, he forced himself to pet dogs, and while doing so to remember these dogs were different than those on the islands where he had fought. This technique helped him to overcome his negative reflexive reactions to innocent animals.

Two weeks after he was discharged, the veteran and his wife were visited by an elderly woman who asked his wife "Why isn't your husband in the army?" That question greatly annoyed the veteran and led him to develop a severe dislike for all elderly women. To conquer such animus, he employed the following two GS notions: *indexing* (elderly woman$_1$ is not elderly woman$_2$ is not elderly woman$_3$, etc.) and *resisting "allness attitudes."*

Finally, the veteran was able to make a more positive readjustment by accepting the Heraclitean idea that the only thing permanent in life is change. The veteran's status had been altered. He was now a civilian not in a battle zone but in the United States where the dangers inherent in combat were no longer present.

The case study ended with these words: "It has been observed by the family of the veteran, and his outside associates, that in the past three months there has been a marked improvement in his attitude and reactions. There is a more general easiness, expressed both in his actions and his physical appearance. The veteran himself admits more confidence in all he undertakes and relief of the absolute tension he previously experienced."[13]

Douglas Kelley did not pursue his efforts in using general semantics to reduce the effects of combat-related PTSD after he left the army following World War II. And, as far as can be gleaned through public documentation, neither has anyone else, which seems a shame as Kelley's and Korzybski's experiences in utilizing GS to mitigate the negative effects of PTSD were quite positive. Given that case, it seems reasonable to suggest that GS should be looked into by researchers and mental health practitioners as an effective modality to treat people suffering from combat-related PTSD.

PART II

GS and Social Concerns

5

General Semantics and Constructive Political Discourse

These days, fighting and frustration characterize many political discussions, as people try to convince others of the rightness of their views and the wrongness of views held by those they are speaking with. Typically they fail in their efforts and wind up feeling angry and discouraged. Better to avoid the topic of politics completely and talk about other things, they surmise, than engage in fruitless dialogue that will only result in ill will and maybe an upset stomach or a rise in blood pressure.

The aforementioned scenario may be true for people not versed in general semantics. But for those in the GS know, such doom and gloom, and the desire to gain the upper hand in political discussions, can be largely circumvented. To that end, this chapter offers the following GS ideas and formulations to employ when having political discussions.

GS Ideas for Constructive Political Discourse

Alfred Korzybski's Happiness Formula

One way to beat the political-discussion blues is to acquaint yourself with Korzybski's "happiness formula": maximum effort + minimum expectations = best results. Maximum effort means understanding that it is important to listen intently to those you are speaking with. If a person feels their ideas are being seriously listened to, they may be more open to considering the ideas of the person with whom they are conversing. Therefore, it makes good sense to put effort into listening to what the other person is saying.

The second part of the formula, "minimum expectations," is as important as the first part. The odds are close to zero that you will sway someone from their entrenched positions in a political discussion. But you may be able to have a civil conversation by responding calmly to arguments being presented to you and by taking those arguments seriously. Sarcasm and self-righteousness tend to put people off, so it is probably best not to employ those communicative forms. Approaching a conversation with a genuine interest and openness to others' perspectives is in most cases a far better way to achieve a true exchange of information and ideas.

The Value of Delayed Evaluation

Alfred Korzybski was fond of pointing out that a key difference between human beings and other animals is the ability we have to engage our higher brain functions and delay long enough to evaluate circumstances before reacting to them. Using this technique tends to produce better outcomes in situations than reacting quickly or impulsively. In the context of political discussions, rather than copy the rapid-fire, in-your-face conversational style of cable TV news hosts in speaking with people, one can pause to think about what the other person is saying and respond in a mindful manner.

Will delaying your reactions win you kudos from a partisan on the opposite side of issues you feel strongly about? It might because, generally, people believe what they are saying is worthy of consideration. But even if you are not commended for your courtesy, not going hell for leather in an argument over politics may spare you and your fellow conversationalist from bodily upset and uttering words you may regret later.

The Limitations of Either-Or Thinking

The law of the excluded middle, one of Aristotle's three "laws of thought," encourages us to believe that every question can be answered in terms of "either-or." The English language pushes us in a similar direction. Its many polarizing terms (e.g., good/bad, hot/cold, tall/short, thin/fat) pushes us to think in extremes rather than with gradations.

Most things we encounter are more accurately mapped by a statistical distribution rather than by either-or terms. This idea can be seen on a bell-curve of normal distribution. If you plot instances from daily life, like days above and below 100 degrees F., I.Q., height, weight, etc., on a graph, it is the middle range that has the most distribution. Either-or comparisons show up at the two extreme ends of the graph.

To get past either-or thinking, general semantics recommends using a *multi-valued approach*. This approach involves examining more than just two alternatives. Rather than arguing immigration is good/immigration is bad, affirmative action is good/affirmative action is bad, defense spending is good/defense spending is bad, a multi-valued approach might involve examining pluses and minuses of various policies regarding immigration, affirmative action, and defense spending. Such analyses may surface ideas one had not reflected on and, at the very least, shed more light than heat on the topic under discussion.

Overcoming "Allness Attitudes"

No one can know *all* about anything. That statement may seem obvious, but everyday people say or imply that they do know it all. Individuals who speak in this manner are demonstrating *allness attitudes*. They think they know what it is impossible to know—everything about a specific topic.

It is hard to talk with people who claim to know everything. They resist any new information you bring to a discussion, so why bother trying to have one. Individuals with allness attitudes do not want to exchange ideas and opinions. They want to pontificate.

Indexing, a GS tool that involves examining individual cases within a larger category, can be useful in overcoming allness attitudes. For example, John says, "I don't like Arabs, Jews, Blacks, and Hispanics." Does John know every Arab, Jew, Black, and Hispanic? $Arab_1$ is not $Arab_2$ is not $Arab_3$; Jew_1 is not Jew_2 is not Jew_3; $Black_1$ is not $Black_2$ is not $Black_3$; $Hispanic_1$ is not $Hispanic_2$ is not $Hispanic_3$. Every human being is unique and the categories we place them in are artificial constructions that do not contain the fullness and distinctiveness of the persons inhabiting that category. Indexing can be a good way to get beyond stereotyping and focus on differences that might make a difference in understanding how particular individuals behave.

Employing qualifying terms like "to me," "I think," and "in my view," when making statements is another general semantics approach for defeating allness attitudes. Such expressions ("To me, X is a great candidate," "I think the Y party is the best one to move America forward," "In my view, the government needs to provide more [or less] student aid") make it clear that our observations and opinions have definite limits.

Finally, we can follow Korzybski's suggestion to add a silent "etc." to our thinking to remind us there is always more that can be learned, more that can be said. When I am engaged in a political discussion I try to remind myself, and those I am speaking with, that when it comes to politics there is more to heaven and earth that can be contained in any person's particular political philosophy.

Differentiating Facts from Inferences

One reason political discussions go off the rail is that the people having them are operating from separate sets of "facts." Can one have a reasonable discussion if the very basis of that discussion is in dispute? Probably not. Does that mean one should walk away from the conversation? Not necessarily.

People often mistake statements of inference for statements of fact. To avoid fact/inference confusion Irving J. Lee, the author of *Language Habits in Human Affairs* and other books on general semantics, offers these distinctions.

Statements of fact
- Made *after* observation or experience
- Is confined to what one observes or experiences
- Only a *limited* number can be made
- Represents a high degree of probability, is close to certainty
- We tend to get agreement when it is possible to make factual statements about an event or situation

Statements of inference
- Made anytime—before, during, or after observation
- Goes beyond what one observes or experiences
- Can make an *unlimited number* in any situation
- Represents some degree of probability
- We can expect disagreement if only inferential statements can be made regarding an event or situation

It may be worthwhile to introduce Lee's distinctions in political discussions and see if everyone can get to agree on the "facts" of the matter. If such agreement is not forthcoming there will likely be difficulty in dialoging, as one party will be talking about apples while the other is speaking about oranges. There can be value in introducing Lee's fact/inference distinctions to those not familiar with them, as they may induce reflection on matters taken for granted. If that's not the case in the near term, they may spur reflection down the road.

Searching for Meaning in the Right Places

What is the difference between a "freedom fighter" and a "terrorist?" Were the victims at the Abu Ghraib prison in Iraq subjected to "abuse" or "torture?" Are organizations that comment on news reporting "media watchdog groups" or are they "pressure groups?" Do not look to the dictionary for the answers to these questions. Their answers depend on how individuals interpret events.

It is an axiom in general semantics that, strictly speaking, words don't "mean," people "mean." The physicist P.W. Bridgman put it this way, "Never ask 'What does word X mean?' but ask instead, 'What do I mean when I say word X?' or 'What do you mean when you say word X?'".[1] The fact is words do not have "one true meaning"—for the 500 most used words in the English language, the *Oxford Dictionary* lists 14,070 meanings.[2] Words mean different things to different people. The field of law is based on this principle.

Words mean different things at different times. In 1896, the nine men on the U.S. Supreme Court said separate but equal facilities for Blacks and whites are constitutional. In 1954, a set of nine different men said, in effect, *separate* and *equal* are opposites.

Words mean different things in different contexts: He beat (hit) the drum with a stick. Beats me (I don't know). The reporter has the mayor on his beat (area to cover.) He beat (defeated) Joe at chess.

We use words to categorize and label people and events. But the categories we formulate are not "out there," in the "real world." They are created in our heads and expressed in language.

How we label or categorize a person, or a situation, will depend upon our purpose, our projections, and our evaluations. North Korea labels itself the Democratic People's Republic of Korea. Vladimir Putin claims that Russian and Ukraine are "one people." Ali Khameni is Iran's "Supreme Leader." Whose purposes do these designations serve?

Putting people into categories is a commonplace occurrence in political discussions on "talk radio" ("You believe that because you're a 'liberal'!" "That's what I though a 'conservative' would say!" "What do you expect from a 'reactionary'!"). Such pigeonholing does not advance political dialogue. Rather it leads to a malady that is rampant in politics: hardening of the categories." The remedy? In political matters, focus on issues not labels.

Conclusion

Many people advise not talking politics in polite company. But at this time in our nation's history, where the political stakes seem existential, there are sound reasons not to follow that advice. If you choose not to follow it, and want to engage with others over politics in a civil and respectful manner, try putting the ideas discussed in this chapter into practice. Good luck and good chatting.

6

Antisemitism: A GS Case Study

On August 16, 1920, while living in New York City, Alfred Korzybski wrote a letter to Cassius Keyser, a professor of mathematics at Columbia University who appreciated the philosophical importance of Korzybski's work. The letter dealt mostly with issues relating to *Manhood of Humanity: The Science and Art of Human Engineering,* a book Korzybski published in 1921 that introduced the idea of human beings as a time-binding class of life. The letter also contained a vicious rant against Jews and their religion. The following are some excerpts from that rant.

. . . . Human = Animal X Spark of god has formed the old testament utterly capitalistic, brutally selfish, with hatred as a base. Every Jew was not human, a beast to be cheated, killed, and so forth. They [the Jews] violated the human nature for centuries. Their theory of selfishness and hatred could not have of course creative inclination. THEY BECAME PARASITES preying upon other people['s] [work]. They are today bankers and merchants, they follow their creed and their culture . . . It happens to be that the Christians are the biggest producers . . . it may happen that Christianity made productiveness, or naturally productive races, accepted the theory of love it means productiveness, no doubt any way that Christianity is strictly related to

61

productiveness. The Jews remained parasites, and they had to be such, the productive element was lacking in them. Selfishness as a creed (in a particularly accentuated form) compelled them to their efforts to accumulate other people's work and be parasites in the newer civilization. Selfishness and greed upon other people's success, in capitalism made them more selfish and greedy, they got in their second stage of their selfish capacity to prey. To prey on the farmer and the poor was not enough. They proclaimed a new creed to prey on the accumulation of dead men's work, to prey on the wealthy and the products of work of brain workers. They do not acknowledge the highest form of binding time, the brain work, practically they prey upon it. . . . Today we see Jewish old testament creed Bolshevism build upon hate and DESTRUCTION (it cannot be different) in Mongol lands [knocking] at the doors of white people christian, love, constructive domain. . . . We are in a stage of confusion here, the very existence of the white race is in danger, only vigorous thinking, Mathematical thinking, binding of time standards can save the Aryan race from the semits [sic] and the Mongols.[1]

More evidence of Korzybski's bigotry against Jews can be found in an article he wrote in 1919 titled "The Profiteers and How to Fight Them." Excerpts of that article, which grossly overstate the economic power of Jews and their ability to act in a joint manner to stifle the Polish economy, appear below:

We had in Poland several years ago a tremendously strong Jewish trust which boycotted for several centuries Polish economic life. Every wholesale dealer in the country was a Jew and every Jewish retailer had the goods cheaper and paid by long drafts, the Christian dealers had to pay dearer and cash.

The situation was hope and helpless. The Jewish Trust was broken by an appeal to the people, who mobilized money and men. Polish wholesale dealers and retailers were established.

The system took away from the Jews the power of exclusiveness and made them equal and not privileged in comparison to the Polish natives. And the fight was won.[2]

Historical Antecedents to Korzybski's Antisemitism

Alfred Korzybski was born in Warsaw Poland, on July 3, 1879. Jews had been living in Poland since at least the Middle Ages and up to the latter part of the 18th century they enjoyed prosperity and relative tolerance. (The rise of Hasidism [a Jewish spiritual and mystical movement] and Haskalah [a Jewish reformation movement] occurred in Poland, and the Polish-Lithuanian Commonwealth was home to most Ashkenazi Jewry into the 18th century.) But in 1772, the relative peaceful coexistence between Jews and Poles was threated when Russia, Prussia, and Austria signed a treaty that partitioned Poland. Most Jews wound up living under Russian rule.

Russia imposed geographic and professional restrictions on Jewish life, confining Jews to a region that came into being under the rule of Catherine the Great in 1791 known as the Pale of Settlement—the archaic English term *pale* is derived from the Latin word *palus*, a stake, such as might be used to indicate a boundary. Warsaw was part of the Pale, and a number of its ethnic-Polish residents viewed the Jews residing alongside them as unwelcome presences in Polish society.

After the assassination of Tsar Alexander II on March 13, 1881 (by a non-Jew), Russian-Polish Jews were exposed to a series of organized massacres called *pogroms* targeting Jewish communities—pogrom is a Russian word that means "to wreak havoc, to demolish violently." Pogroms against Jews had happened before, but the pogroms that began in the 1880s were the first to assume the nature of a mass movement. In December 1881, a Warsaw pogrom left 2 dead, 24 injured and lots of Jewish families financially ruined. In the months afterwards, about a thousand Warsaw Jews emigrated to the United States.[3]

In 1903, a fabricated antisemitic text titled *Protocols of the Elders of Zion* was published in Russia. It described a Jewish plot for global domination and included plans to subvert the morals of the non-Jewish world, plans for Jewish bankers to control the world's economies, plans for Jewish control of the press, and ultimately plans for the destruction of human civilization. As the Russian Revolution unfolded, many "White Russians" escaped to the West, some bringing copies of the *Protocols* with them. Soon after, editions popped up across Europe, the United States, South America, and Japan. In 1920, the first English edition of the *Protocols* was published in Great Britain.

Between 1880 and 1920 over two million Eastern European Jews, most of them destitute and fleeing from pogroms, religious persecution, and poor economic conditions, came to the United States. Many Americans looked askance at these people with their alien traditions and Yiddish accents. One of those Americans was Henry Ford.

In 1918, Ford purchased his hometown newspaper, *The Dearborn Independent*. A year and a half later, he authorized publication of a series of articles that claimed a vast Jewish conspiracy was corrupting America—the series ran in the following 91 issues. Ford had the series bound into four volumes titled "The

International Jew" and distributed half a million copies to his nationwide network of auto dealerships and subscribers. He also arranged for the republication of the *Protocols of the Elders of Zion*, a book Korzybski was aware of through a mention of it in the 1919 Overman Committee report to the US Senate on the influence of Bolshevism in America.[4]

During World War I, Korzybski served as an intelligence officer with the Russian army, a military force whose commanders were overtly antisemitic, which led to Jews being expelled from their homes in areas near the front lines, having their movements restricted, and being taken as hostages as a way of instilling fear and submission in the rest of the Jewish population. In 1916, after being wounded in a leg and suffering other injuries, Korzybski moved to North America (first to Canada then to the United States) to coordinate artillery shipments to Russia. When the war ended, he decided to stay in America where he worked on developing a system to promote sane human evaluating.

Korzybski's anti-Jewish prejudice was most likely influenced by the antisemitic culture and world he had grown up in and the antisemitism taking place in the United States at the time he came to America in 1917. Bruce I. Kodish, Korzybski's biographer, suggests influences on Korzybski's bigoted attitude toward Jews include his contact with Social Credit advocates, some of whom believed in a conspiracy of Jewish bankers against the public; contact with US Army and State Department personnel who believed in a Jewish-Bolshevik conspiracy; and contact with Boris Brasol—a cultured Russian émigré who was a proponent of the *Protocols of the Elders of Zion*.[5]

Given the antisemitism rife in postwar America, and Korzybski's interactions with people promoting antisemitism, the fact that Korzybski espoused antisemitic views does not seem all that unusual. What does seem unusual is that by the spring of 1921

Korzybski was showing evidence of what Kodish labels a kind of "philosemitism"—a respect for Jews and Jewish culture.

A Reevaluation

According to Kodish, Korzybski's attitudinal change toward the Jews and their religion was based on serious research and contact with individuals who brought new information about Jews and Judaism to the table. Such information led Korzybski to understand that: Jews were not the bulk of the radical and communist groups that wanted to overthrow the US government; that the "conspiratorial Jewish marriage of capitalism and communism"—Jews controlling both Bolshevism and the banks—was false; that a Jewish plot of world domination, as was detailed in the *Protocols of the Elders of Zion*, was untrue; and that there was much to be learned from Simon Wolf's introductory remarks to the Overman Committee, which are detailed below:

> I am not at all surprised by the accusations against a certain portion of the human family entitled the Jewish . . . always made the scapegoat of every movement. It has been so from time immemorial. I am also reminded of the Irishman who beat the Jew and when asked why he did so said that he had killed Christ. When the answer came that had been done thousands of years ago, the Irishman replied that he had never heard of it until that day.
>
> And again, when a Jew was walking down the street, a stone was thrown from the opposite side. Naturally the Jew dodged and the stone went crashing into the plate-glass window. The owner sued the Jew for damages and the judge decided that the Jew must pay, for had he not dodged the window would not have been broken. . . . the misfortune is

that the Jew throughout all history has been dodging those kinds of missiles and subjected to such unjust decisions.[6]

In going through Korzybski's papers for work on his biography, Kodish found evidence of Korzybski's study of Jewish history, religion, and philosophy. One example was the discovery of a page in Korzybski's notebook devoted to Jewish libraries, publishers, and communal organizations in New York City. Kodish also unearthed, in the Korzybski archives housed at Columbia University, several pages of notes with extensive annotated lists of diverse sources of Hebrew literature and history, including translations of the Talmud (the central text of Rabbinic Judaism) and the Kabbalah (Jewish mystical literature). Many of the books Korzybski acquired on Jewish subjects became part of the Institute of General Semantics Library.

Korzybski took copious notes on Richard J.H. Gottheil's *Zionism* (1914), a book that details the history of modern political Zionism, a movement that sought to reestablish a substantial Jewish presence in the land of Israel. Korzybski's reading of that book might have marked the beginning of his support for Zionism. Some evidence of that support can be found in 1929 when two Jewish newspapers in Kansas City Missouri, where Korzybski was speaking at The Young Men's and Young Women's Hebrew Association, declared him "an outspoken Zionist" in articles announcing his lecture. Korzybski did not renounce that label. He seemed proud of it, clipping the articles and writing positively to friends about the enthusiastic newspaper coverage."[7]

From 1921 on, Korzybski evinced a concern about antisemitism and talked and wrote about Judaism and the Jewish people with compassion. During the 1920s, in letters to his friend A.A. Roback (a Jewish-American psychologist and proponent of Yiddish), Korzybski would often ask in a kind manner about the ethnicity of various Jewish mathematicians and scientists. Kodish writes that "[Korzybski] came to feel that the Jews as a group, like the Poles and the Scots, had especially developed a 'time' or process orientation foreshadowing the modern way of thinking he wanted to formulate more clearly . . . The Jewish people constituted the only ethnic or religious group (including the Poles) about whom Korzybski ever published anything specific . . ."[8]

In 1943, Korzybski published a foreword to "The Essence of Judaism,"[9] an article written by Hans Kohn (a Prague-born, Jewish historian) that had been run in *The American Scholar* in the spring of 1934—the article presents a clear distinction between the stagnant, "space" orientation of ancient Greek civilization (which, in GS terms might be labeled "Aristotelian") and the dynamic, "time" orientation of Jewish civilization. Korzybski arranged to have his foreword, and a reprint of Kohn's article, published and distributed by the Institute of General Semantics.

Korzybski was an outspoken critic of the Nazis, condemning their ideology and their persecution of the Jews. In his foreword to "The Essence of Judaism" he says, "In the present world crisis and the German efforts to exterminate the Jews, the issues involved here become sharper in perspective, showing clearly the German cultural regression to ancient barbarism, following the sick semantic deterioration of a few leaders. From a cultural point of view, what was standard 2,000 or 3,000 years ago, if inflicted on modern civilization today must be considered regressive in the psychiatric sense, and therefore pathological like any other kind of modern gangsterism."[10] In a letter to his friend, the psychiatrist Philip Graven, Korzybski writes, "one cannot profess Gen. Sem. and not perceive the horrors of Hitlerism. You know he hates the Jews. All of us as persons have perfect right to select their friends, but these personal attitudes should never be generalized. The issue is fundamental for us and between us. PLEASE read carefully in the American Scholar, Spring, 1934, an article by Kohn 'The Essence of Judaism'. With some revision of language what he says is profoundly true, but applies not only to Jews but to many individuals in every nation . . ."[11]

In a chapter in his Korzybski biography titled "Alfred and the Jews," Kodish says that "Korzybski's efforts at self-education regarding Jews and Judaism reflected an all too rare but much to be wished for condition . . . "[12] That much to be wished for condition led Alfred Korzybski's views on antisemitism(pre 1920) to be quite different from Alfred Korzybski's views on antisemitism(post 1920).

Korzybski's willingness to question his bigoted beliefs about Jews and Judaism, and his willingness to seek more information and insight into those beliefs, lends support to the idea that there can be worth and importance in reevaluating one's biases. Such reevaluation may help to create in the "re-evaluator" a saner and more reality-based outlook toward groups they may have prejudged. In these times of rising global antisemitism,[13] reexamination of negative Jewish stereotyping seems particularly needed and is something all fair-minded individuals might consider promoting.

7

Judicial Bias, Meaning and the Law

What's wrong with these statements?: "The Second Amendment says the government can't infringe on the right of people to bear arms." "The law declared at one time that slaves were property, and Blacks were noncitizens." "Laws against drugs cry out their meanings in ways easily understood." The answer is laws don't talk. They are words on paper, or screens, inanimate and incapable of producing sounds.

Judges produce sounds, and written opinions, and the sounds and written opinions they produce in rendering decisions determines what the law is. Judges are like ventriloquists speaking for the law, which can be thought of as a puppet having its strings pulled. The meanings of laws are not in the laws themselves. Their meanings lie in the decisions of judges, or as practitioners of general semantics might put it, meanings are in people not in words.

That meanings are in people was clear to me as a first-year law student in 1968, and the idea led me to suggest that while studying the law was all well and good, there ought to be a law-school class devoted to studying the judges that were ruling on the law to see if there were any personal biases that swayed them in their rulings. It seemed to me judges, like every other human being I had met in my life, were susceptible, knowingly or unknowingly, to bringing their prejudices and predispositions to bear on the work they did.

There are countless illustrations of how the personal biases of judges affect their decision in cases. In 1857, in a shameful case that stunned the nation (*Dred Scott v. Sandford*), the Supreme Court, led by Chief Justice Roger Taney, ruled 7-2 that slaves were property and that Blacks, including freedmen, were not citizens. Through this decision Black people, wherever they lived, were reduced to the status of commodities.

The Taney court was dominated by pro-slavery judges from the South. Of the nine justices, seven had been appointed by pro-slavery presidents and five had come from slave-holding families. Chief Justice Taney had characterized the abolitionist movement as one of "Northern aggression."

Two justices raised in the North dissented in the Scott case. Justice John McLean of Ohio concluded that there was nothing in the Constitution that required someone born in the United States to do anything more to become a citizen. Justice Benjamin R. Curtis of Massachusetts opined that the argument Scott was not a citizen was "more a matter of taste than of law," saying Black men were not only considered citizens but they could vote in 5 of the 13 states at the time. Their arguments did not win the day. The Scott case was a triumph for the Slaveocracy and showed the power the South had over the highest court in the country.

In 1896, the Supreme Court declared in *Plessy v. Ferguson* (1896) that racial segregation laws did not violate the Constitution if the facilities for each race were equal in quality, a policy that came to be known as "separate but equal." The 7-1 decision legitimized the many state laws that had reestablished racial segregation in the South after the end of Reconstruction and opened the floodgate for Jim Crow legislation.

The one dissenting justice in the case, John Marshall Harlan, accused the majority of being "willfully ignorant" of the purposes of the Louisiana law they were ruling on—that law required "equal but separate" accommodation by race on railway cars. He argued that *everybody knew* the purpose of the Louisiana law was not to exclude whites from railroad cars occupied by Blacks, but the other way around. He said the Constitution was colorblind and with respect to civil rights, all citizens were equal before the law.

Most legal scholars believe the seven Supreme Court Justices who ruled the Louisiana law constitutional knew, *like everyone else* at the time, the purposes of that law and like many in the country viewed whites as socially superior to Blacks. With the end of Reconstruction, the country had stopped paying much attention to conditions in the South with respect to race relations and people had stopped caring much about how Blacks were being treated. These considerations were likely in the minds of the justices who voted to uphold racial segregation in the Plessy case, whose "separate but equal" doctrine remained the law of the land till 1954 when the Supreme Court reversed itself on the matter with their 9-0 ruling in *Brown v. Board of Education.*

Bush v. Gore (2000) was a Supreme Court case in which, for the first time in American history, the court decided who would be the next President of the United States. In proceedings lasting just two days, the Court determined it was a violation of the Equal Protection Clause to count uncounted votes in Florida without clear, uniform standards. The justices split 5-4, entirely on ideological lines. Many legal scholars and Gore supporters felt the ruling was a partisan decision where five Republican justices gave the election to the Republican candidate, George W. Bush.

Lots of Americans thought the verdict smacked of political favoritism, as a good number of the Republican lawyers representing Bush had clerked for the Court's Republican justices and had worked for right-wing special-interest groups that had put pressure on loyalists, like Justice Clarence Thomas, to influence the Court's conservatives. Prior to the case, these conservatives had consistently argued for federalism and states' rights, a judicial philosophy that if applied would have resulted in remanding the case to the Florida courts. The dissenting justices referenced that last point in their published opinion, citing the hasty about-face the conservative justices made in jettisoning a position they had previously strongly espoused.

The judgment of the Court stopped the ballot-counting, with George Bush in the lead by just a few hundred votes. Many people felt if Gore rather than Bush had been in the lead the Court would have allowed the vote counting to go on. Justice John Paul Stevens in his dissent concluded that the nation would never know for sure who had won the 2000 presidential election, but the loser was clear. It was the nation's confidence in the judge as an impartial arbiter of the rule of law.

With respect to judges being impartial determiners of the law, a 2017 article in the Florida Law Review titled *Judging Implicit Bias: A National Empirical Study of Judicial Stereotypes,* (69 FLA. L. REV. 63) described an empirical study that tested this notion. The study looked at 239 sitting federal and state judges (including 100 federal district judges representing all Circuits) and examined the ways in which judicial implicit biases may manifest in court cases. The findings showed the judges harbored strong to moderate negative implicit stereotypes against Asian-Americans and Jews, while holding favorable implicit stereotypes towards whites and Christians. These negative stereotypes associated Asians and Jews with immoral traits, such as "greedy," "dishonest," and "controlling," and associated whites and Christians with moral traits, such as "trustworthy," "honest," and "giving." The study also found that federal district court judges sentenced Jewish defendants to marginally longer prison terms than identical Christian defendants and that implicit bias was likely the cause of the disparity. The authors said their study suggested that automatic biases and cognitions influenced a much broader range of judicial decisions than had previously been considered.

In 2022, the Supreme Court held in *Dobbs v. Jackson Women's Health Organization* that the Constitution does not confer a right to abortion. The court's decision overruled both *Roe v. Wade* (1974) and *Planned Parenthood v. Casey* (1992), returning to individual states the power to regulate any aspect of abortion not protected by federal law.

Linda Greenhouse, a journalist who covers the Supreme Court and the law for the *New York Times*, argued that religious doctrine and not the law drove the Dobbs decision, whose renunciation of Roe was affirmed by five justices raised in the Catholic church. There was only one Catholic justice on the court in the case that decided Roe.

Greenhouse noted that in the 79-page majority decision there are a great deal of highly partial and substantially irrelevant accounts of the history of abortion's criminalization and very little actual law. Critics of Dobbs have said that the Court's decision privileges religion over nonreligion, which is itself unconstitutional, and privileges the life of the fetus over the life of the mother. They claim it's a case in which religious morality prevailed over secular law.

Roe was doomed when three Catholic, anti-abortion leaning justices were appointed to the Supreme Court during the presidency of Donald Trump—as a candidate Trump had pledged to end Roe through his appointments of Supreme Court justices. Trump chose the three justices from a list of candidates supplied by the Federalist Society, a group committed to overturning Roe. The Dobbs decision is a textbook case of how the religious biases of judges can impact the law.

Another case involving religion influencing judicial decision making is *Burdick-Aysenne et al v. Center of Reproductive Medicine* (2023), an Alabama Supreme Court case that, in an 8-1 decision, elevated human embryos to the status of children for the purpose of wrongful death lawsuits. In his "special concurrence," Chief Justice Tom Parker argued that human life cannot be wrongfully destroyed without incurring the wrath of a holy God, who views the destruction of his image as an affront to himself. Parker said that even before birth all human beings bare the image of God, and their lives cannot be destroyed without effacing his glory—the word "God" appears 41 times in Parker's opinion along with quotes from the Bible and Christian theologians such as St. Thomas Aquinas and John Calvin. Parker's comments in the Burdick case are an example of a government official backing Christian nationalism, a movement that seeks to privilege Christianity and merge Christian and American identity.

Since first elected to the nine-member court in 2004 and in his legal career before it, Parker has been transparent in voicing how his Christian beliefs have significantly formed his understanding of the law and his approach to it both as a lawyer and a judge. Whatever one may think of Parker's vote in the case, to his credit Parker wears his religious biases on his black-robed sleeve. Such transparency among judges is rare, which is why in 1968 I argued the merits of having a class in law school devoted to uncovering judicial bias in legal decisions. It never happened but for the record I still think it's a good idea.

PART III

Dating Change Over Time

8

Dating American Disunity

There is a widespread feeling today among many Americans that, given the huge amount of political discord and harsh rhetoric going on between Republicans and Democrats, the United States should call itself "The Disunited States of America." In point of fact, that's an idea that could have been proposed many times in our nation's history, as Americans have been at loggerheads politically since the founding of the Republic.

This chapter will examine political disunity in the United States using the general semantics device of dating—attaching dates to our evaluations to remind us that change occurs over time. Specifically, nine different time periods when national disunity was particularly evident will be explored. Let's begin with the first period, when America was still a British colony.

Dating Nine Periods of American Disunity

American Disunity(Pre and Post the Revolutionary War)

It is impossible to know the exact number of American colonists who favored or opposed independence. But there were individuals who identified themselves as "Loyalists" (people partial to England and King George), "Patriots" (people who wanted independence from England and the king), and persons not wanting to take a stand on independence. Fortunately, for the cause of independence, the Patriots were the most successful group in drawing support—Committees of Correspondence persuaded many fence sitters to join the patriot movement and works such as Tom Paine's *Common Sense* did too.

Patriots subjected Loyalists to public humiliation and violence. Loyalists had their property vandalized, looted, and burned. Bad things occurred to those who publicly professed sympathy for Britain and the crown.

General Benedict Arnold was one of the most famous Loyalists. Other well-known Loyalists included the governor of the Massachusetts Bay Colony, Thomas Hutchinson; Joseph Galloway, the Pennsylvania delegate to the First Continental Congress; the mayor of New York City, David Mathews; and Benjamin Franklin's son William, the governor of New Jersey.

When the Revolutionary War ended many Loyalists left America, going mainly to England or Canada. American history labels them as "traitors." But most were just trying to sustain lifestyles to which they had become accustomed. Had the British won the war, Washington, Adams, and Jefferson would have been seen as traitors. But the winners write history so Washington, Adams, Jefferson, and America's other Founding Fathers, are called heroes. To the victors belong the (linguistic) spoils.

American Disunity(1796 and 1800)

Political factions began to form during the fight over the ratification of the federal Constitution of 1787. Friction between them increased as attention shifted from the formation of a new federal government to the question of how powerful that federal government would be. The Federalists, led by Treasury Secretary Alexander Hamilton, wanted a strong central government. The Anti-Federalists, led by Secretary of State Thomas Jefferson, backed the notion of states' rights over centralized power. The ensuing partisan battles led George Washington to warn of "the baneful effects of the spirit of party" in his Presidential Farewell Address.

The election of 1796 was the first election in American history where political candidates at the local, state, and national level ran for office as members of organized political parties. John Adams was the Federalist Party candidate in the presidential race. Thomas Jefferson, running as a Democratic-Republican (the name suggests the party wanted to extend the Revolution to ordinary citizens) opposed Adams.

The election was waged with great intensity. The Federalists charged the Democratic-Republican Party's advocacy of democracy would bring mob rule, like the French Revolution. The Democratic-Republicans said the Federalists wanted to establish a monarchy. Adams wound up narrowly winning in the Electoral College, 71 to 68.

The election of 1800, a bitter, contested rematch between Adams and Jefferson, marked the first time political power was transferred from one party to another. Adams was accused of wanting to be a king and starting a dynasty by having his son succeed him. He was also mocked for being overweight and given the nickname "His Rotundity." Jefferson was accused of having an affair with one of his female slaves and running away from British troops during the Revolution. Adams did not bother attending Jefferson's inauguration. The two men did not speak to each other for twelve years after that.

Adams and Jefferson died on the same day, July 4, 1826, one in Massachusetts, the other in Virginia, one 91, the other 83, on the 50th anniversary of the Declaration of Independence. By then their political animosity toward each other had long since been forgiven and forgotten. Adams' last words were, "Thomas Jefferson still survives."

American Disunity(1812)

In the War of 1812, the United States once again fought the British and their Indian allies. Some historians see the conflict as a second war for American independence. The war itself was mostly a political and military disaster for the nation.

The US Congress was far from unanimous in its declaration of war—almost four in ten members of the House voted against the measure. In the summer of 1812, America invaded Canada (then ruled by England). Tecumseh and the British repulsed the American forces. Due to domestic discord, the US was unable to remount another invasion of Canada—one reason for this was the governors of most New England states refused to allow their state militias to join a campaign beyond state boundaries.

In December and January of 1814 and 1815 respectively, twenty-six Federalists representing New England states met at the Hartford Convention to discuss how to stop the decline of their party and the region. Although manufacturing was booming and contraband trade brought much wealth to the area, "Mr. Madison's War" and its expenses were an abomination to New Englanders.

Holding this meeting during the war was controversial. Some attendees at the convention called for New England to secede from the United States. That call was voted down, but most Democratic-Republicans considered the Hartford Convention an act of treason. If a peace treaty ending the War of 1812 had not been signed while the Hartford Convention was still in session, the citizens of New England may have seriously considered leaving the Union.

American Disunity(1828)

The election of 1828 pitted the incumbent, John Quincy Adams, against an angry Andrew Jackson who believed he had won the presidential election of 1824. In that race, Jackson won the popular vote but lost to Adams in the Electoral College. After the 1824 election, Jackson's supporters immediately began making plans for a second go round.

The 1828 election included strong personal attacks on each of the candidates. Jackson's supporters accused Adams of having had premarital sex with his foreign-born wife and living in "kingly pomp and splendor." Adams was also accused of misusing public funds—he had supposedly purchased gambling devices for the presidential residence. In fact, he had simply bought a chessboard and a pool table.

Adam's supporters attacked Jackson as being uneducated and reckless and said that he and his wife Rachel were adulterers. (Rachel was a divorcee and she and Jackson believed that her divorce was finalized before their marriage. The papers were incomplete, however, and Jackson's political opponents publicly branded her an adulteress. Mrs. Jackson was humiliated by the accusations, became ill, and died before the inauguration. Jackson believed the personal attacks against his wife caused her death and said, "May God Almighty forgive her murderers as I know she forgave them. I never can.")

Amidst all the mudslinging, Adams lost the election in a landslide. He was so upset over his defeat that he didn't attend Jackson's inauguration. Like his father, John Adams, he snuck out of the capital and went home.

Jackson's inauguration seemed to many the epitome of mob rule by detestable rapscallions. Jackson rode to the White House followed by a horde of well-wishers who were asked in. Muddy boots tromped on new carpets, glassware and crockery was demolished; men stood on expensive upholstered sofas trying to get a glimpse of the new president. To stem the destruction, Jackson ordered the punch bowls moved to the White House lawn, and the crowd followed. Jackson's critics referred to his inauguration party as the beginning of the "reign of King Mob."

Jackson has been widely revered as an advocate for democracy and the common man. But many of his actions proved divisive. Such actions included signing the Indian Removal Act, which forcibly removed most major tribes of the Southeast to Indian Territory; opposing abolition, threatening to use force if South Carolina seceded from the country, and dismantling the National Bank.

In 1834, those who disagreed with Jackson's expansion of executive power united and formed the Whig Party to take on "King Andrew I." They named their party after the English Whigs, a group opposed to the British monarchy in the 17th century. The Whigs in the Senate proposed a motion that would censure Jackson in the upper chamber. It was ratified and Jackson responded by issuing a lengthy protest denying the validity of the censure. Although many people feared the Union would not survive Jackson's presidency, America did not disintegrate. Rougher times lay ahead.

American Disunity(1860)

The Democrats met in Charleston, South Carolina, in April 1860 to select their candidate for President in the upcoming election in November. It was bedlam. Northern Democrats argued that Stephen Douglas, a strong backer of slavery, had the best shot to defeat the "Black Republicans." But Southern Democrats thought Douglas a traitor because of his support of popular sovereignty, which could enable territories to ban slavery within their borders. Southern Democrats stormed out of the convention, without choosing a candidate. Six weeks later, the Northern Democrats chose Douglas, while at a separate convention the Southern Democrats chose then Vice President John C. Breckenridge.

The Republicans met in Chicago that May and recognized the Democratic Party's turmoil would make it much easier for the Republican nominee to win the election. They needed to pick a candidate who could carry the North and be victorious in the Electoral College. There were lots of possible candidates, but in the end Abraham Lincoln, a one-time US representative from Illinois, got the nod.

A number of former Whigs, mostly from the south, who wanted to sidestep the slavery issue and not join either the Whigs or the Democrats, formed the Constitutional Union Party, which nominated John Bell of Tennessee, a wealthy slaveholder, to be their candidate for President. With four entrants in the field, Lincoln received a shade under 40% of the popular vote and 180 electoral votes, which was enough to narrowly win the general election. More than sixty percent of the voters selected someone other than Lincoln. The question became, would the South accept the result? Six weeks after the election, South Carolina seceded from the Union.

American Disunity(1865-1877)

For freed slaves, Reconstruction offered an extraordinary window of hope. Blacks could now vote and own property. In parts of the South, they could ride with whites on trains and dine with whites in restaurants. Schools, orphanages, and public relief projects aimed at improving the lives of Black people sprang up in various places. African-Americans were able to hold political office, becoming sheriffs, judges, school board members, and city councilmen—sixteen Blacks sat in Congress from 1865-1877 and about 600 served as legislators on the local level.

But economically, Blacks remained an underclass. Most had skills best suited for plantation work. By the early 1870s, sharecropping became the leading way for former slaves and poor white farmers to earn a living.

Contracts between landowners and sharecroppers were typically harsh and restrictive. Many contracts forbade sharecroppers from saving cottonseeds from their harvest, which forced them to increase their debt by obtaining seeds from the landowner. Sharecroppers often found themselves in debt, as they had to borrow on bad terms and pay dearly for supplies. Often a sharecropper's debt exceeded their harvest revenues, which bound them to their lenders. In many ways, this system resembled slavery.

Lots of whites resented the changes going on around them. Taxes were high, the economy was listless, and corruption ran rampant. Carpetbaggers, northerners who saw a chance to get rich fast by gaining political office that was barred to the old order, were a source of annoyance and anger. Scalawags, southern whites who supported Republicans and Reconstruction-era policies, were considered as bad or worse than carpetbaggers.

Out of a mix of anger and fear, the Ku Klux Klan and the Knights of the White Camelia emerged. These white supremacy guerilla groups sought to control African-Americans through violence and intimidation. Looting, lynching, rape, and terror were commonplace.

For many emancipated Blacks, the new order did not look very inviting. Poll taxes, violence at the ballot box, and literacy tests kept Blacks from voting. Pressure to go back to the plantations increased. Slavery had ended but the struggle for equality had just begun.

American Disunity(the 1930s)

Franklin Roosevelt's New Deal era policies were ambitious, far-reaching, and had numerous supporters. But they also had enemies. Liberals and radicals attacked from the left saying FDR's policies did not offer enough relief and kept the basic aspects of capitalism in place. Conservatives claimed FDR's policies were socialistic and were destroying an American tradition of self-reliance.

Sensible Thinking 3

Father Charles E. Coughlin, a priest who used radio to reach a mass audience (his show reached up to 30 million people) was a particularly influential Roosevelt critic. Originally a New Deal supporter, Coughlin turned against Roosevelt for being a friend of Wall Street and for recognizing the Soviet Union. Coughlin had an isolationist, and conspiratorial, viewpoint that resonated with many of his listeners. As the decade progressed, Coughlin became openly antisemitic, blaming the Great Depression on a conspiracy of Jewish bankers. In November 1934, Coughlin formed the National Union for Social Justice, which served as the foundation for the formation of a third political party. That party broke up following Roosevelt's reelection in 1936.

In 1937, frustrated by a conservative Supreme Court overturning New Deal initiatives, FDR announced a plan to expand the Supreme Court. He proposed that when a federal judge reached the age of seventy and failed to retire, the president could add an extra justice to the bench. His scheme would immediately enable him to appoint six justices to the high court.

Conservative Democrats and Republicans charged FDR with abuse of power and did not support the plan. During the 1938 Congressional elections, Roosevelt actively campaigned against anti-New Deal Democrats. In almost every case, the conservatives won. This coalition of Southern Democrats and Republicans controlled the Congress until the 1960s and effectively ended the reform spirit of the New Deal.

Many denounced FDR's running and winning a third term in 1940. In 1944, he went on to win a fourth term, serving only 82 days before he died. The passage in 1951 of the 22nd Amendment that limited the number of terms served by a US Chief of State was a reaction to Roosevelt's serving 12 years in office.

American Disunity(1968)

The turbulent 1960s hit a boiling point in 1968. When the year began, President Johnson hoped to win the war in Vietnam and then a second term to complete his plans for the Great Society. But events worked against him.

In February, the Tet Offensive shifted American public opinion on the war and brought low approval ratings for Johnson. In March, Senator Eugene McCarthy, a peace candidate who had entered his name into four Democratic primaries in 1967, won 42 percent of the vote in the New Hampshire primary. Johnson understood that strong result portended that his road to the Democratic presidential nomination would not be an easy one. That road became significantly harder when Robert Kennedy threw his hat into the ring in mid-March.

On March 31, 1968, Johnson announced he would not seek a second term. His Vice-President Hubert Humphrey entered the race to carry out Johnson's programs.

Political turmoil escalated in the spring. Humphrey was popular among party elites who chose delegates in many states. But Kennedy was waging an inspiring campaign. And both Kennedy and McCarthy were critical of Humphrey's hawkish stance on Vietnam.

On April 4, Martin Luther King was assassinated. This led to a wave of civil unrest, perhaps the greatest unrest the nation had seen since the Civil War. On June 6, an assassin killed Kennedy. The killing traumatized the nation and many concluded that violence had become endemic in American society.

There was a Democratic Convention in Chicago that August. With Kennedy out of the race, the nomination of Hubert Humphrey was a given. Antiwar protestors gathered in Chicago to prevent the expected Humphrey nomination, or to at least to pressure the party into moderating its position on Vietnam.

Mayor Richard Daley ordered the Chicago police to stand tough against the protestors. As the crowds chanted, "The whole world is watching," the police attacked the activists with clubs and tear gas. The party nominated Humphrey, but the nation began to sense that the Democrats were a party that was becoming unhinged.

The Republicans had a comparatively smooth convention, nominating Richard Nixon as their candidate. Nixon spoke for the "Silent Majority" of Americans who supported the war in Vietnam and demanded law and order. Alabama Governor George Wallace ran on the American Independent Party ticket, campaigning for "segregation now, segregation forever," a notion that appealed to many white voters in the South. His running mate, Curtis Lemay, suggested bombing Vietnam "back to the Stone Age."

In the November election, Nixon won just 43.4 percent of the popular vote but cruised to an Electoral College landslide. When he ran for president four years later, he won even more votes in the Electoral College and garnered almost 61 percent of the popular vote. Two years after that, brought down by his role in the Watergate scandal, Nixon resigned from the presidency and, in a highly controversial decision, was given a full and unconditional pardon for any crimes that he might have committed against the United States by his successor, Gerald Ford.

American Disunity(the 1990s)

Bill Clinton entered the White House in 1992 after beating an incumbent Republican president and having a Democratic Congress in place. He seemed to have everything going for him but early in his term a health care plan assembled by a task force headed by his wife was defeated in Congress by conservatives who said the plan was socialist and too costly. It didn't help Clinton that powerful interest groups were also against it.

The Republicans won the House and Senate in the 1994 midterms and Clinton pledged to work with the new leadership. House Majority Leader Newt Gingrich and his associates had other ideas. (In 1990, Gingrich had issued a memo in which he urged Republican candidates to use "optimistic, governing words" like "opportunity," "courage," "pristine," and "principled" to describe themselves and words like "betray," "cheat," "corrupt," "lie," "sick," and "traitor" to describe their Democratic opponents. Some believe Gingrich's hyper-partisan political rhetoric mark the beginning of the massive incivility evident on the political scene today.)

In 1995, the Republicans shut down the government when Clinton would not go along with their cuts to social spending. The public blamed them for the shutdown and Clinton was easily reelected in 1996.

In January 1998, a scandal surfaced that nearly ended Clinton's presidency. It was reported that Clinton engaged in a sexual relationship with a White House intern named Monica Lewinsky during his first term. Although Clinton initially denied the charges, overwhelming evidence was presented that he and Lewinsky engaged in repeated sexual contact.

Republicans were outraged. An independent counsel was appointed to gather evidence against Clinton. As the summer ended, Clinton admitted many of the reports were true and he was ashamed of his behavior. The House Judiciary Committee drew up four articles of impeachment. Across the nation, Americans debated whether Clinton's misconduct rose to an impeachable offense.

The House went forward with two articles of impeachment and in December 1998, Clinton joined Andrew Johnson as the only US presidents to be impeached. Clinton survived his trial in the Senate through a vote that split along party lines. Polls indicated most Americans thought the impeachment harmful to the country.

As the year 2000 approached, partisan politics were as noxious as ever. Republicans claimed that they had fixed the economy and Clinton got the credit. Democrats said "Clintonomics" (a portmanteau of "Clinton" and "economics") was responsible for the strong economic growth in the 1990s. The century ended with the nation's two major political parties poles apart on a host of issues and, with increased attention being paid to social media outlets and partisan cable news channels, that situation has gotten a lot worse.

Conclusion

The United States was born in discord and the tendency toward political disputation has never disappeared. With that said, America has endured, and its constitutional provision of checks and balances is still functioning. Whether that will be the case in the future is anybody's guess. But if past is prologue there is a good chance that if enough Americans want the Republic to continue, and work on keeping democratic norms and institutions in place, the Republic will live on.

Dating America's Response to Alcohol

In 2002, I published a book titled *The Drug Problem: A New View Using the General Semantics Approach* (Praeger) that contained a chapter which used the general semantics dating technique to help understand how and why American attitudes and policies toward heroin, cocaine, marijuana, opium, morphine, LSD, amphetamines, and barbiturates had changed over the course of US history. I've always regretted not having included alcohol in the drugs I reviewed. This chapter makes up for that omission.[1]

Dating America's Response to Alcohol

America's Response to Alcohol(1620-1776)

The passengers on the Mayflower were rationed a gallon of beer a day on their voyage to the New World, and as they neared Plymouth Rock their supplies were running low. Beer was a main source of hydration in the 17th century (drinking water was unsafe), and the captain of the Mayflower wanted to ensure there would be enough beer for his sailors. So he told the ship's passengers to disembark and get the lay of the land.

In 1630, the ship that brought John Winthrop to the Massachusetts Bay Colony carried more than ten thousand gallons of wine on board and three times as much beer as water. The

Puritans were not going to make the same mistake the Pilgrims did with respect to having ample supplies of alcohol available for consumption. Likewise Harvard College, which one year after its founding in 1635, was developing plans to build a brewery on its campus. Having access to alcohol was clearly valued by the early English colonists in America.

In 1737, Benjamin Franklin published a list he devised of 228 terms for the term "drunk," a state of intoxication that was pretty common among the colonists, in the *Pennsylvania Gazette*. One way to get sloshed was to imbibe hard cider, a beverage made from apples and other fruits crushed and fermented in homes across the land. Downing distilled liquor was also a popular choice—in 1763, 159 commercial distilleries were distilling rum in New England alone.

Penalties for drunkenness included being put into stocks (where the locals would often throw food or stones at the lawbreaker), having to pay a fine, being forced to wear the letter "D" around your neck, and having one's name posted over the door of a tavern. The colonists struggled to define drunkenness and, as blood alcohol testing was not available, it was up to a magistrate to decide whether an inebriated defendant had been drunk.

In 1755, George Washington lost his first campaign to the House of Burgesses because he did not supply enough booze to voters at the polls. He did not make the same mistake three years later and the result was he won his election. (Washington enjoyed a variety of alcoholic beverages, his favorites being sweet, fortified wines like Madeira and Port. He also drank rum punch, porter, and whiskey.)

The average colonist spent a quarter of his income on alcohol. Drinking commenced from the time a person got up for breakfast in the morning to the time they went to bed at night. Most colonists began the day with a drink, often a mug of cider or a mixture of rum and hard cider. Infants were given rum for sleep, workers took drinking breaks during the day, and drinking in taverns was commonplace.

British excise taxes on foreign molasses, a key ingredient in the making of rum, spurred a colonial smuggling trade. The colonists were partial to rum as, besides liking its taste, the alcohol content of rum was higher than beer or cider and it didn't spoil as fast as those beverages. By the time of the Revolution, Americans were among the world's heaviest drinkers.

America's Response to Alcohol(1776-1840)

During his iconic ride, Paul Revere stopped at Hall's Tavern in Medford to have a couple of drinks to give him strength. When the British confronted a company of militiamen in Lexington the following morning, they were also facing men who had spent the previous night drinking, and bellyaching about the British, inside Buckman Tavern. At Valley Forge, George Washington insisted to the Continental Congress that his men's rum ration be doubled and throughout the Revolutionary War he did what he could to supply his troops with spirits.

In the early days of the Republic, drinking was part of the warp and woof of everyday life. Children drank before school, farmers swigged from jugs stashed in their fields, and factory workers consumed alcohol during drinking breaks. By 1820, the average amount an individual drank in one day was more than three times the average today.

Some did not look kindly on alcohol, particularly its effects on people who could not hold their liquor. Lyman Beecher, a Presbyterian minister and the father of the novelist Harriet Beecher Stowe, was leery of alcohol. In his *Six Sermons on Intemperance* he argued that only total abstinence could help people who could not control their drinking. In 1829, there were around 1,000 temperance societies in America. Those numbers increased greatly during the 1830s, a time when drinking in the United States reached its highest point since the landing of the Pilgrims.

With the development of a temperance movement, drinking in America began to decrease. Some, following the lead of Doctor Benjamin Rush, began to view alcoholism as a disease. (In 1784, Rush published a landmark pamphlet titled "An Enquiry into the Effects of Spirituous Liquors Upon the Human Body and Their Influence Upon the Happiness of Society" that suggested alcoholism was a chronic illness, one that got progressively worse as the person became more addicted to drink. Rush also suggested that alcoholism has a genetic component and can be passed down generationally within families.) Some temperance groups practiced compassion rather than coercion to get their message across to those who were still drinking.

The Washingtonians, a group from Baltimore that showed up in a popular novel by Timothy S. Arthur titled *Ten Nights in a Bar-Room and What I Saw There*, was one of the earliest and most powerful temperance groups. They held meetings where reformed drunks told their stories of battling alcohol to try to get more men to take the pledge. Despite some early successes, by the Civil War their program had mostly dissipated due to criticism of the program for not claiming alcohol was a moral failing, for having some of its members continue to get drunk despite their pledge, for allowing tavern keepers to become members of the group, and for allowing discussion of controversial social and political concerns such as prohibition, sectarian religion, and the abolition of slavery.

Walt Whitman and P.T. Barnum were proponents of temperance. The Good Gray poet rarely drank—his first novel *Franklin Evans* (1842) was a rags-to-riches temperance tract. P.T. Barnum, "America's Greatest Showman," was a teetotaler and a strong supporter of temperance. Barnum was a highly effective temperance speaker, giving speeches across America on the evils of alcohol.

In the 1830s, more than a million people took the "pledge," which meant abstaining from certain kinds of hard liquor and not becoming overly intoxicated. Tens of thousands also took a "teetotaler pledge." It seemed people were moving from being constantly buzzed to wanting to go in a more sober direction.

America's Response to Alcohol(1840-1920)

By 1840 the temperance movement was booming. Ministers and doctors took the pledge and encouraged their congregants and patients to do the same. A desire for religious salvation and material gain had become imbued in the culture and temperance was well-suited to both these yearnings. Recreational drinking began to be thought of as infra dig.

By 1860, drinking had become a shameful practice in many quarters of society. However, that was not true for soldiers fighting in the Civil War. For many of them drinking often began as soon as they were away from home. The Union's top general, Ulysses S. Grant, was a binge drinker whose penchant for drink was usually kept in check by his adjutant. Of the more than 75,000-recorded courts-martial conducted by the Union Army during the Civil War, almost twenty percent were for drinking or drinking-related infractions.

Those who went West in the nineteenth century were often men in search of a new kind of life, and drinking was one way to keep one's spirits up during hard times—it was also one way to keep one's spirits up during easy times and times when nothing was going on. Saloons served trappers, cowboys, soldiers, businessmen, lumbermen, lawmen, miners, and gamblers. Politicians also frequented saloons to curry favor with potential voters.

Women did not patronize saloons. For the most part women drank at home, many drinking patent medicines that contained alcohol. *Peruna*, a well-known patent medicine, contained 28 percent alcohol. *Hostetter's Celebrated Stomach Bitters* contained 47 percent alcohol—more than an average whiskey.

In the latter half of the 19th century, two powerful temperance groups sprang up—the Woman's Christian Temperance Movement (WCTU) and the Prohibition Party. At its founding in 1874, the WCTU announced its purpose was to create a "sober and pure" world through abstinence, purity, and evangelical Christianity. Its constitution called for "the entire prohibition of the manufacture and sale of intoxicating liquors as a beverage."

The WCTU grew rapidly. Its most famous member, Carrie Nation, a Kansas minister's wife, led bands of women into saloons where they sang hymns to the patrons and told bartenders "Good morning, destroyer of men's souls!" Nation would sometimes enter bars and after singing and praying, smash their fixtures and stock with a hatchet. The press labeled such actions "hatchetizations."

The Anti-Saloon League (ASL) began life as a state organization in 1893. In 1895, it went national and quickly morphed into the main player in the temperance movement.

The ASL was the first modern pressure group in the United States organized around a single issue. It lobbied at all levels of government for legislation to ban the manufacture or importation of spirits, beer, and wine. Its most prominent leader was Wayne Wheeler, who developed a method of activism that came to be known as "Wheelerism," an approach that relied heavily on mass media to persuade politicians to back ASL positions. Wheelerism also included direct persuasion of those in power through tactics such as threats to withdraw campaign endorsements, financing and supporting opponents, and revealing embarrassing information to get support for liquor trade restrictions.

The efforts of the WCTU, the Prohibition Party, and the ASL to prohibit the sale and manufacture of alcoholic intoxicants were met with success on January 16, 1919, when the 18th Amendment to the Constitution was ratified. The amendment declared the production, transport, and sale of intoxicating liquors illegal. Shortly afterwards, Congress passed the National Prohibition Act (known informally as the Volstead Act), which provided for federal enforcement of Prohibition.

America's Response to Alcohol(1920-1933)

A day before the Volstead Act went into effect, on January 16, 1920, the popular evangelist Billy Sunday held a mock funeral for John Barleycorn in Norfolk, Virginia. At the service he said, "The reign of tears is over. The slums will soon be a memory. We will turn our prisons into factories and our jails into storehouses and corncribs. Men will walk upright now, women will smile and the children will laugh. Hell will be forever for rent." It didn't turn out that way.

The Volstead Act did not prohibit the consumption of alcohol. It made the manufacture, importation, sale, and transport of alcohol illegal. The challenge for the federal government was how to get people to comply with the law.

Three federal agencies were assigned the task of enforcing the Volstead Act: the Treasury Bureau of Prohibition, the Coast Guard Office of Law Enforcement, and the Department of Justice Bureau of Prohibition. Enforcement was more vigorously pursued in places where people liked the idea of prohibition (e.g., rural areas and small towns) and more loosely in places where they didn't (e.g., urban areas).

"Bootlegging," the illegal manufacturing and sale of liquor, was widespread during the Prohibition Era, as was the operation of "speakeasies" (stores or nightclubs that sold alcohol). There was also the smuggling of alcohol across state and international borders, and the informal manufacture of liquor in private homes.

Before the 1920s, criminal organizations and gangs concentrated their operations on prostitution, gambling, and theft. Prohibition expanded the scope of black-marketeering to illicit alcohol. Gangster chiefs like Al Capone raked in up to $100 million a year thanks to the illegal booze trade.

Prohibition had a negative impact on the American economy by causing billions of dollars of lost tax revenues from the non-sale of alcohol. It also led to the shutdown of distilleries, breweries, and liquor stores and the loss of jobs in alcohol-related fields (e.g., barrel making, trucking, glass-making, and the hospitality industry).

Bootleg alcohol could be toxic and was sometimes expensive, so a number of drinkers switched to opium, cocaine, marijuana, patent medicines, and other dangerous substances. Many stills used lead coil or lead soldering, which gave off acetate of lead—a dangerous poison. Some bootleggers added iodine, creosote, or even embalming fluid. The result of such adulteration could be paralysis, blindness, and occasionally death.

Some people drank industrial alcohol. Knowing this, in 1926, the federal government increased the amount of methanol, a poisonous alcohol-based substance, required in industrial alcohols. The increase was meant to dissuade people from drinking. But many drank the further-poisoned alcohol. Thousands died as a result.

When the Great Depression hit, potential tax revenue from alcohol sales became an appealing idea to financially struggling municipalities, states, and the federal government. Lots of people liked the notion that revenue from alcohol sales might lead to a reduction in income tax rates. As disillusion and dissatisfaction with Prohibition spread, and as the economy worsened, organizations like the Association Against the Prohibition Amendment, the

United Repeal Council, and the Women's Moderation Union began to push harder for prohibition reform.

On March 22, 1933, President Franklin Roosevelt signed the Cullen-Harrison Act (an amendment to the Volstead Act) that allowed the manufacture and sale of 3.2% beer and light wines. The Volstead Act previously defined an intoxicating beverage as one with greater than 0.5% alcohol. People gathered outside breweries and taverns to celebrate the Act.

A little less than nine months later, on December 5, 1933, the 21st Amendment, which repealed the 18th Amendment, was ratified by the requisite number of states. "The Noble Experiment," which was undertaken to reduce crime and corruption, decrease the tax burden created by prisons and poorhouses, solve social problems, and enhance health in America was over. But not completely. The 21st Amendment did not infringe on state or local temperance laws and though Prohibition was repealed on the national level, eighteen states maintained prohibition and about two-thirds of all states provided for local options whereby residents of counties and other political subdivisions could vote on the issue. But in most places alcohol was legal again. The nation had tried prohibition and found it wanting.

America's Response to Alcohol(1933-present)

Following the repeal of Prohibition, home consumption of beer was made easier with the spread of home refrigerators and the arrival of the aluminum can in 1934. Hotels and restaurants capitalized on the popularity of cocktail drinking by opening sophisticated cocktail lounges that could attract women as well as men. To add some panache, the old term "bar room" was avoided. In its place were labels such as cocktail bars, cocktail lounges, Persian rooms, palm rooms, and taprooms. "Cocktail hours" were promoted to boost patronage.

The need to treat alcoholics continued to be a problem. In 1934, the newly abstemious Bill Wilson met detoxing alcoholic Dr. Bob Smith in Akron, Ohio. Wilson told Smith that alcoholism was not a failure of will or morals, but an illness that he had recovered from as a member of the Christian revivalist Oxford Group. Smith became a founding member of Alcoholics Anonymous, which was officially formed in 1935. That same year, the American Medical Association (AMA) recognized alcoholism as a disabling physical condition requiring treatment.

During World War II, distillers produced industrial alcohol for the war effort and cut down on whiskey production. This led to the increased popularity of rum imported from the Caribbean. Beer drinking was also popular. The US government directed the brewing industry to allocate fifteen percent of its products for the military to ensure beer could be had by the troops.

In the 1950s, alcohol drinking was a staple at cocktail parties held in newly built homes in suburbia. Drinking cocktails was part of the decade's lifestyle image, as was drinking beer. In 1952, the American Psychiatric Association (APA) designated alcoholism as part of a subset of personality disorders in the first-edition of the *Diagnostic and Statistical Manual of Mental Disorders.*

Alcohol use continued apace in the 1960s. Heavy drinking was common among men, and a drinking problem wasn't a problem. As the decade wore on, the APA began to urge health insurance companies to start covering alcoholism, and they began to comply.

In 1970, Congress passed the Comprehensive Alcohol Abuse and Alcoholism Prevention, Treatment, and Rehabilitation Act, which created the National Institute on Alcohol Abuse and Alcoholism (NIAAA). Since 1974 the NIAAA has been an independent Institute of the National Institutes of Health, studying issues relating to alcohol and health.

In 1980, Mothers Against Drug Driving (MADD) was established to reduce alcohol-related fatalities. Four years after that the National Minimum Drinking Age Act was passed, which made 21 the legal age for drinking in the US. In 1988, Congress passed a bill requiring health and safety warnings on all alcoholic containers.

The 1990s saw the rise of pub and club culture and the arrival of new kinds of alcoholic drinks aimed at youths known as "alcopops"—sweet, often fruit-flavored alcoholic drinks, closely resembling soda or energy drinks and containing up to 12% alcohol.

In 2000, Congress required states to establish a maximum blood alcohol concentration (BAC) for operating motor vehicles at 0.08 under penalty of loss of federal highway funds for failure to comply with the directive. The measure saved lives that would otherwise have been lost to driving under the influence. But many lives are still being lost to drinking.

From 1999 to 2017, the number of alcohol-related deaths in the US doubled to more than 70,000 a year. And the numbers may get worse. During the pandemic, drinking frequency rose, as did the sale of hard liquor. Today, some supermarkets have beer and wine-bars, and alcohol is showing up in places it hasn't been before like movie theaters, drive-throughs, vending machines, and coffee shops.

With more venues available for drinking, will drinking become a bigger problem than it already is? Given America's up and down history with alcohol, perhaps the best answer to that question is "it's hard to say."

10

Dating Western Poetry

Alfred Korzybski, the author of *Science and Sanity* and the originator of general semantics, valued more than just the language of science and math. He had a great respect for the arts and, in fact, was married to the distinguished portrait painter, Mira Edgerly. As for poetry, he wrote the following in *Science and Sanity*: " . . . it is well known that many scientists, particularly the creative ones, like poetry. Moreover, poetry conveys in a few sentences more of lasting values than a whole volume of scientific analysis."[1]

This chapter, which surveys over 3,000 years of Western poetry, aims to provide some sense of where poetry has been and where it is going using the general semantics device of *dating* (attaching dates to our evaluations to remind us that change occurs over time). Nine time periods are discussed, and examples given of some of the finest poems and poets of each period. The current state of Western poetry is also examined, and a forecast is given about its future.

Dating and Surveying 3,000 Years of Western Poetry

Western Poetry(1000 BCE-400 BCE)—The Biblical/Homeric Period

More than half of the Old Testament is poetry, a form that allowed its writers to express spiritual truths in powerful and striking ways. The following is a poetic passage from the book of *Ecclesiastes* (31:5) that is imbued with balance, clarity, and grandeur. A rock version of these lyrics reached the number one spot on the *Billboard Hot 100* chart in 1965.

> For everything there is a season
>> and a time for every matter under heaven:
> a time to be born, and a time to die;
> a time to plant, and a time to uproot;
> a time to kill, and a time to heal;
> a time to break down, and a time to build up;
> a time to weep, and a time to laugh;
> a time to mourn, and a time to dance;
> a time to cast away stones,
>> and a time to gather stones together.

The word Homeric refers to Homer, the presumed ancient Greek author of the *Iliad* and the *Odyssey,* two epic poems that are the foundational works of Greek literature. Aristotle annotated a copy of the *Iliad* for his student Alexander the Great who carried it with him wherever he went. Homer's poetry not only influenced literature but also ethics and morality through lessons contained in his writings, which are still widely read by modern audiences.

Western Poetry(750 BCE-676 CE)—The Classical Period

The classical period was home to the great literary and art works of ancient Greece and Rome. A number of scholars say the Greek poets set a standard for creativity and excellence that has never been equaled. One of the earliest and best of these poets is Sappho, an archaic poet from the island of Lesbos. In the following poem, which reflects the conventions of early Greek poetry, particularly its focus on beauty and eroticism, she tells a woman she's in love with that she envies the man sitting next to her sweetheart.

He is more than a hero

He is a god in my eyes—
the man who is allowed
to sit beside you—he

who listens intimately
to the sweet murmur of
your voice, the enticing

laughter that makes my own
heart beat fast. If I meet
you suddenly, I can't

speak—my tongue is broken;
a thin flame runs under
my skin; seeing nothing,

hearing only my own ears
drumming. I drip with sweat;
trembling shakes my body

and I turn paler than
dry grass. At such times
death isn't far from me

Virgil, one of Rome's most important classical poets, drew from his studies of the *Iliad* and the *Odyssey* to help him create *The Aeneid*, the national epic poem of ancient Rome that traces the adventures of Aeneas, the legendary founder of Rome. Virgil's work has had wide influence in Western literature, most notably in Dante's narrative poem *Divine Comedy*, in which Virgil appears as the author's guide through Hell and Purgatory. Other important Latin classical poets include Catullus, who wrote poetry to his treasured Lesbia; Horace, who replaced Virgil as the poetic voice of the state and who was perhaps the greatest of all Latin lyricists; and Ovid, whose *Metamorphoses*, a narrative poem containing Greek and Roman myths, is considered one of the most influential works in Western culture, inspiring authors such as Dante, Boccaccio, Chaucer, and Shakespeare.

Western Poetry(476-1000)—The Dark Ages

The idea of the so-called "Dark Ages" came from Renaissance scholars like Petrarch, who viewed ancient Greece and Rome as the pinnacle of human achievement. But lots of good poetry was written in this "Dark" period. In Europe, most of that poetry was in Latin.

The most famous Dark Ages poem is *Beowulf*, an epic poem that was scripted anonymously. (A significant amount of medieval literature is anonymous. This is not only owing to an absence of documents from the period, but also because the view of the author's role in medieval times differed considerably from the romantic understanding in use today.) The following is a passage from *Beowulf*:

To him was conceived an heir in days after,
young in the yards, whom God had sent
as a comfort to the people—he understood the dire
 distress
they had suffered before, bereft of a king
for a long while. Therefore the Lord of Life,
the Sovereign of Glory, gave to them worldly honor.

Beow was famous—prosperity sprang widely—
as Scyld's son, throughout all the northern lands.

Beowulf contains 3,182 alliterative lines, mostly written in a dialect of Old English, that deal with events of the early 6th century. It has influenced many other works, including graphic novels and comics, opera and theater compositions, video games, and the *Lord of the Rings* trilogy. *Beowulf* is one of the most significant and most translated works of Old English literature.

Western Poetry(1000-1450)—The Middle Ages

In Europe, the Middle Ages were dominated by the Catholic Church and its official language, Latin. But many European poets were beginning to write in their native vernaculars. In France, there was the epic battle poem *The Song of Roland.* Germany produced courtly love and chivalric romances like *Parsifal* and *Tristan and Isolde.* In England, Geoffrey Chaucer penned the English masterpiece *The Canterbury Tales.* Italy was represented by perhaps the finest poet of the age, Dante, who wrote the epic religious poem *The Divine Comedy* (see excerpt below), wherein the speaker takes a guided tour through Hell, Purgatory, and Paradise:

In the midst of the road of our lives,
I found myself on a darkened path
   With the right way lost,
Ah! It is so hard to say how savage
And bitter and rough that road was
   That as I think of it, the fear returns.

Other major works from the Middle Ages include *The Poem of the Cid* (the national epic poem of Spain), the *Song of the Nibelungs* (Richard Wagner's operatic cycle *Der Ring des Nibelungen* is based on the Old Norse version of the Nibelung saga), and *Carmina Burana,* a manuscript collection of 254 poems.

Western Poetry(1450-1674)—The Renaissance

The Renaissance was a time of rebirth of interest in the Greek and Latin writers. It started in Italy, where great epic poems emerged, moved to France, and traveled north. Spain experienced a prolific period of dramatic poetry. Lope de Vega is probably the best-known Spanish Renaissance poet. In France, Racine, Corneille, and Molière wrote dramatic poems.

The English Renaissance produced writers such as Shakespeare and Sir Walter Raleigh, but many first-rate poets were working in England as well. A number of poetic forms extant today were born in the English Renaissance: Blank verse (unrhymed iambic pentameter) was the form Shakespeare and many of his fellow dramatists wrote their plays in. Ballad forms were used in folk poetry, songs, and madrigals. Sonnets (intricately rhymed 14-line poems) were penned in most of the major European languages.

In 1650, Anne Bradstreet, America's first published poet, came out with a book of poems titled *The Tenth Muse, Lately Sprung Up in America* that was widely read in America and England. In one of her poems, "Letter to her Husband, absent upon Publick Employment," she writes about her longing to be with her partner who is away at work. The poem is notable for its candid description of female desire and its use of extended metaphors and personification: The following is an excerpt.

I weary grow, the tedious day so long;
But when thou *Northward* to me shalt return,
I wish my Sun may never set, but burn
Within the Cancer of my glowing breast,
The welcome house of him my dearest guest.

Where ever, ever stay, and go not thence,
Till natures sad decree shall call thee hence;
Flesh of thy flesh, bone of thy bone,
I here, thou there, yet both but one.

Despite heavy criticism of women writers at the time, Bradstreet continued to write. Her work has endured. Bradstreet is the first poet listed in *The Oxford Book of American Verse* and her straightforward way of turning the everyday experience of family and self into verse foreshadowed the future of poetry in America.

Western Poetry(the 18th century)—Enlightenment Poetry

The eighteenth century was dominated by an intellectual movement known as the Enlightenment, which emphasized reason and individualism rather than tradition. A characteristic form of the age was the "essay poem," of which *An Essay on Criticism* by Alexander Pope is an example. In this poem, Pope gives an explanation in heroic couplets of what poetry is and how it works. Memorable lines include: "To err is human; to forgive divine," "A little learning is a dang'rous thing," and "For fools rush in where angels fear to tread." Jonathan Swift, John Dryden, Samuel Johnson, and Alexander Pope are important Enlightenment poets.

Western Poetry(the 19th century)—Romantic, Victorian, and Modern American Poetry

Three developments marked the 19th century with respect to poetry: Romanticism, Symbolism, and the beginning of modern American verse.

Romantic poetry involved a reaction against the fundamental Enlightenment ideas of the 18th century. It brought a revolution in the kind of language poets used. Odes were popular and because of the emphasis on sincerity and emotion, *lyric poems* became the foremost genre, which it continues to be to this day. Many poets wrote sonnets and some wrote epic poems that centered on personal subjects rather than public events. Notable Romantic poets include Robert Burns, William Blake, Lord Byron, William Wordsworth, Percy Bysshe Shelley, and John Keats. The following is an excerpt from Keats's *Ode to Melancholy*.

> She dwells with Beauty—Beauty that must die;
>   And Joy, whose hand is ever at his lips
> Bidding adieu; and aching Pleasure nigh,
>   Turning to poison while the bee-mouth sips:

Symbolist poets tried to evoke states of feeling through their poetry, rather than detailing precisely what their poems meant. Symbolist poems were built on striking, intuitive associations. Symbolist poets influenced many prominent 20th century poets, among them Rainer Maria Rilke, William Butler Yeats, Wallace Stevens, T.S. Eliot, and Adrienne Rich. The following stanza from *Memory*, by Arthur Rimbaud, is an example of symbolist poetry:

> Longing for thick, young arms of pure grass!
> Gold of April moons in the heart of the holy bed! Joy
> Of abandoned woodyards by the river, prey
> To August nights that made the rotten things sprout!

Walt Whitman, a latter-day successor to Homer, Virgil, Dante, and Shakespeare, is one of the most influential poets in the American canon. His *Leaves of Grass*, a book comprising mostly long-lined open form poems, is noteworthy for its discussion of delights in sensual pleasures during a time when such portrayals were deemed immoral. The poetry in *Leaves of Grass* is an unreserved celebration of the world and one's place in it, qualities very much in evidence in the following Whitman poem:

Spontaneous Me

Spontaneous me, Nature,
The loving day, the mounting sun, the friend I am
    happy with,
The arm of my friend hanging idly over my shoulder.
The hillside whiten'd with blossoms of the mountain ash,
The same late in autumn, the hues of red, yellow, drab,
    purple, and light and dark green,
The rich coverlet of the grass, animals and birds, the
    private, untrimm'd bank, the primitive apples, the
    pebble-stones,
Beautiful dripping fragments, the negligent list of one
    another as I happen to call them to me or think
    of them

Whitman's expansive poetry went beyond traditional meter and stanza forms commonplace in poetry during the previous 1,300 years. "The Good Gray Poet"—as his disciple William Douglas O'Connor dubbed him—paved the way to modern American poetry. Ezra Pound called Whitman "America's poet," saying that "He is America."

Emily Dickinson, a writer the literary critic Harold Bloom listed among the 26 central writers of Western civilization, wrote short, trenchant poems that experimented with rhyme and form. She often punctuated her poems with dashes, rather than periods, commas, and other standard punctuation marks. She also capitalized interior words, not just words at the start of a line. The following poem, *I'm Nobody! Who are you?* is characteristic of Dickinson's poetic style.

I'm Nobody! Who are you?
Are you - Nobody - too?
Then there's a pair of us!
Don't tell! they'd advertise - you know!
How dreary - to be - Somebody!
How public - like a Frog –
To tell one's name - the livelong June –
To an admiring Bog!

Western Poetry(the 20th century)—The Modern and Post-Modern Eras

The early 20th century saw a reaction against formal structure and style. Free (or open-form) verse became more popular and there was added interest in realism. The Irish poet William Butler Yeats transformed himself from a romantic poet to a modern one with poetry that was more colloquial, politicized, and direct. Yeats's modernist poem *The Second Coming*, which is about political demagoguery, contains lines that have become famous like: "Things fall apart, the centre cannot hold," "The best lack all conviction, while the worst are full of passionate intensity," and "What rough beast, its hour come round at last, slouches towards Bethlehem to be born?"

Ezra Pound, one of the most influential poets of the 20th century, wrote poetry that concentrated on the *image* (a focused moment of revelation, epiphany, or complex feeling). His poems show the occasion for emotion but do not delve into it. Pound's "verbless" poem, *In a Station of the Metro*, which appears below, is considered one of the leading poems in the Imagist tradition.

The apparition of these faces in the crowd;
Petals on a wet, black bough.

Marianne Moore is known for her meticulously detailed poems about animals, subjects she frequently employed as central images to emphasize themes of individuality, honesty, and the mixing of art and nature. Her work is often associated with poets such as H.D., William Carlos Williams, Wallace Stevens, and Elizabeth Bishop. The following stanza from Moore's poem *The Monkeys* is characteristic of her style.

The Monkeys

Winked too much and were afraid of snakes. The zebras, supreme in their abnormality; the elephants with their fog-colored skin and strictly practical appendages were there, the small cats; and the parakeet —trivial and humdrum on examination, destroying bark and portions of the food it could not eat.

T.S. Eliot utilized many literary and cultural allusions from the Western canon, Buddhism, and the Hindu Upanishads to create *The Waste Land*, perhaps the most important poem of the 20th century. Like Yeat's *The Second Coming*, Eliot's poem is one of intense horror (see below):

Who are those hooded hordes swarming
Over endless plains, stumbling in cracked earth
Ringed by the flat horizon only
What is the city over the mountains
Cracks and reforms and bursts in the violent air
Falling towers
Jerusalem Athens Alexandria
Vienna London
Unreal

The French poet, André Breton, helped create *Surrealism*, a 20th-century avant-garde movement in art and literature that sought to release the creative potential of the unconscious mind. Breton outlined the aims of surrealism in his *Surrealist Manifesto* (1924), affirming the supremacy of "disinterested play of thought" and the "omnipotence of dreams" rather than reason and logic. The following is a passage from *A Man and Woman Absolutely White*, a Breton poem illustrative of Surrealism.

> Deep under the parasol I see the marvelous prostitutes
> On the side near the streetlamps their gowns the color of
>   polished wood
> With them they walk a big piece of wallpaper
> At which one cannot look without that choking feeling on
> The ancient floors of a house under demolition
> Where a slab of marble lies fallen from the fireplace
> And a net of chains is tangled in the mirrors

The Postmodern period (the second half of the 20th century) was marked by irony and social commentary. Postmodern poetry includes such modes as conceptual poetry, cyberpoetry, and conceptualism, which often involve appropriation and cyber sampling. Notable postmodern poets include Amiri Baraka, Robert Lowell, Frank O'Hara, Sylvia Plath, Anne Sexton, and Allen Ginsberg whose opening lines from his poem *Howl* appears below.

> I saw the best minds of my generation destroyed by
>   madness, starving hysterical naked,
> dragging themselves through the negro streets at dawn
>   looking for an angry fix,
> angelheaded hipsters burning for the ancient heavenly
>   connection to the starry dynamo in the machinery
>   of night,

who poverty and tatters and hollow-eyed and high sat up
smoking in the supernatural darkness of cold-water
flats floating across the tops of cities contemplating jazz,

Around 1970, poets began to write what became known as *feminist poetry*—verse that explores the lives of women and how social conventions of society affect women. There was also feminist experimental verse, in which poets examined the idea that there may be unique feminist ways of expanding poetry's horizons to provoke deeper levels of thought.

Experimental poetry had been around earlier in the 20th century. An example is Pierre Reverdy's poem *Departure* (see below), written in 1919. Reverdy's verse compresses the feelings of taking a trip into language resembling a Cubist collage.

The horizon slips down
The Days are longer
Trip
A heart hops in a cage
A bird sings
It will die
Another door will open
At the end of the hall
Where a star
Flares up
A dark-haired woman
The lantern of the departing train

Performance poetry is poetry specifically composed for or during a performance before an audience. During the 1980s, the term came into popular use, as poets across the world began to read their work in public. Performance poetry typically is delivered in strong dramatic ways and may include acting out parts of a poem, changing the reciting speed from slow to fast or the other way around, and pausing to create tension.

Poetry slams, competition arts events in which poets perform their work before a live audience and a panel of judges (often the audience itself) began in the US in the 1980s when open mic sessions started at cafés in major American cities. They are a break from viewing poetry as an elitist or rigid art form. While setups can vary, slams are typically loud and lively, with audience participation and dramatic recitations. Today, poetry slam competitions are ubiquitous, occurring in countries around the globe.

Western Poetry(2000-the present)—The Connected Era

In the Connected Era, forms are mingling with each other to create all kinds of amalgams. There is poetry that rhymes and poetry that doesn't. Prose poetry, a type of writing that combines the lyrical and metric elements of traditional poetry with elements of prose, such as standard punctuation and no line breaks, has become quite popular in the Connected Era. Performance poetry is also popular, running close to written poetry as the foremost poetic form of the age.

Performance poetry has had a long history in the United States. Amy Lowell, who devoted her life to the cause of modern poetry, spoke the following lines of poetry over a hundred years ago in an address she gave to the Poetry Society of America at the National Arts Club in New York City.

From *Spring Day*

Bath

The day is fresh-washed and fair, and there is a smell of tulips and narcissus in the air.

The sunshine pours in at the bath-room window and bores through the water in the bath-tub in lathes and planes of greenish-white. It cleaves the water into flaws like a jewel, and cracks it to bright light.

Little spots of sunshine lie on the surface of the water and dance, dance, and their reflections wobble deliciously over the ceiling; a stir of my finger sets them whirring, reeling. I move a foot, and the planes of light in the water jar. I lie back and laugh, and let the green-white water, the sun-flawed beryl water, flow over me. The day is almost too bright to bear, the green water covers me from the too bright day. I will lie here awhile and play with the water and the sun spots. The sky is blue and high. A crow flaps by the window, and there is a whiff of tulips and narcissus in the air.

In the 21st century, poetry continues to be an important force in the world and, with the rise of Instagram poetry and poetry appearing in other digital venues, it is arguably being enjoyed by more readers than ever. While poets still write about love, war, and death, there is added interest now in reading or hearing poems about the environment, sexual harassment, and empowerment. A constant in the poetry scene is the ubiquity of the lyric poem, wherein poets can express their personal emotions and feelings.

The form, or forms, poetry will take in the years ahead is unknowable. But we know Western poetry has been around for more than 3,000 years and it seems vigorous and growing. If past is prologue, there is a strong likelihood that poetry will continue to evolve and develop in the years to come.

Part IV

The Map is Not the Territory

11

Mapping Language and Rhetoric from the Vietnam War

"You can kill ten of my men for every one I kill of yours.
But even at those odds, you will lose and I will win."
—Viet Minh leader Ho Chi Minh in a warning
to French colonialists in 1946.

Wars between nations are not just fought with munitions. They are also fought with language and rhetoric that try to sway perceptions and win people over to one's cause. That certainly was the case in the *Vietnam War*, a conflict that occurred in Vietnam, Laos, and Cambodia from 1955 to 1975.

The North Vietnamese did not call it the Vietnam War. They labeled the fight *The American War* or *The Resistance War Against America,* as the United States was perceived to be the aggressor. Before the Vietnam War, the Vietnamese had battled the French in a war generally known as the *Indochina War* or *Dirty War* in France and the *Anti-French Resistance War* in Vietnam.

When the French were defeated in 1954 at the Battle of Dien Bien Phu, they withdrew from Vietnam. The *New York Times* reported that "About 94,000 French troops died in the war to keep Vietnam, and the struggle for independence killed, by conservative estimates, about 300,000 Vietnamese fighters."[1] So began what some have labeled *The Second Indochina War*, a war that started because the Eisenhower Administration opposed the 1954 Geneva Accords, which called for future national elections to unify the country. Those elections held the possibility that communists could rule Vietnam.

Language and Rhetoric of the Vietnam War

The Eisenhower Administration

President Eisenhower was determined to not let communists govern Vietnam because of his belief in *containment,* a Cold War policy designed to stop the spread of communism, and his faith in the *domino theory*—a policy that suggested that a communist government in one nation would rapidly lead to communist takeovers in neighboring states, each falling like a perfectly aligned row of dominos "[that would result in the] loss of Indochina, of Burma, of Thailand, of the Peninsula, and Indonesia . . ."[2] And so America supported a South Vietnamese government that did not allow a vote on the unification of Vietnam.

The excuse that the South Vietnamese government gave for not holding a unification vote was that South Vietnam was not a party to the Geneva Accords. This was technically true, as South Vietnam did not exist at the time the Accords were signed. The Republic of South Vietnam was created a year later in 1955.

Eisenhower deployed a US Military Assistance Advisory Group (MAAG) to train the army of the newly formed state, and he lauded its President, Ngo Dinh Diem. He said Diem, who told his US advisors that he had received 98.2% of the vote in the presidential election, was "an example for people everywhere who hate tyranny and love freedom."[3] That certainly was not the case for Buddhists in South Vietnam, a group that Diem, who led the Catholic faction of the country, persecuted. When Eisenhower left office in January 1961 the US had approximately 1,000 military advisors in South Vietnam.

The Kennedy Administration

President Kennedy, like Eisenhower, thought the US needed to contain communism. In his inaugural address, delivered on January 20, 1961, he said, "Let every nation know, whether it wishes us well or ill, that we shall pay any price, bear any burden, meet any hardship, support any friend, oppose any foe, in order to assure the survival and the success of liberty."[4]

During his tenure as president, Kennedy signed the Foreign Assistance Act of 1962, which permitted military assistance to countries on the rim of the Communist world and under direct attack. He furnished the South Vietnamese government with helicopters and fighter planes, along with the pilots to fly them, and gave consent to the use of napalm bombing, free-fire zones, and defoliation using the herbicide Agent Orange. Kennedy authorized the CIA to encourage a group of South Vietnamese generals to depose President Diem—a man Kennedy thought did not have the support of his people and could not defeat the communists. The coup that followed led to Diem's assassination in November 1963 and from that time to the end of 1965, at least eleven governments came and went in South Vietnam, none lasting very long, even with US backing.

Kennedy appointed Robert S. McNamara, the president of the Ford Motor Company, as his defense secretary. In April 1962, he sent McNamara, who Kennedy called the smartest man he had ever met, to assess the situation in South Vietnam. After returning from the trip McNamara said, "Every quantitative measurement that we have shows we are winning the war."[5] His statistical analysis indicated the military mission could be completed in three or four years. At the time of Kennedy's assassination, in November

1963, there were roughly 16,000 military advisors serving in South Vietnam.

The Johnson Administration

After Kennedy was assassinated, Lyndon Johnson became president, and he too relied heavily on McNamara's advice to win the war. McNamara stayed in his defense post for seven years, longer than anyone since the job's creation in 1947. He became the most influential defense secretary of the 20th century.

On August 4, 1964, President Johnson went on national television and told the nation that the North Vietnamese had attacked two US naval vessels in the Gulf of Tonkin and that reprisal raids were underway in response. He stated to the viewing audience that the US sought no wider war.

On August 5th, in a message to Congress, LBJ said he would be asking for a Congressional resolution to express the unity and determination of the United States to support freedom and protect peace in Southeast Asia: "This is not just a jungle war, but a struggle for freedom on every front of human activity."[6] The Resolution specifically authorized the President to do whatever was necessary to assist any member or protocol state of the Southeast Asia Collective Defense Treaty. This included involving armed forces.

On August 7th, the Tonkin Gulf Resolution was passed by a unanimous affirmative vote in the House of Representatives and a vote of 88-2 in the Senate. Before casting his "no" vote, Oregon Senator Wayne Morse, who voted against the Resolution because he thought Article I of the Constitution would be violated if Congress surrendered its authority to check presidential power, said, "I believe that within the next century, future generations will look with dismay and great disappointment upon a Congress which is now about to make such a historic mistake."[7] (A report declassified by the National Security Agency in 2005, showed the

August 4th attack never happened. The American ships had been firing at radar shadows on a dark night.)

During the 1964 presidential election campaign, Barry Goldwater, the Republican nominee, charged that Johnson had lied to the American people and was committing the United States to war "recklessly." He described the war as "Johnson's War" and said if the United States was not prepared to "take the war to North Vietnam" it should withdraw. Two weeks before the election, in a speech at the University of Akron, Johnson said, "We are not about to send American boys nine or ten thousand miles away to do what Asian boys ought to be doing for themselves."[8] A little over four months later, on March 2, 1965, Johnson initiated *Operation Rolling Thunder*, a massive bombing campaign of North Vietnam that would eventually result in the flying of more combat sorties than the combined number of US, British, and French sorties flown in World War II.

On March 8, 1965, two battalions of US Marines, the first American combat ground forces that were not advisors, disembarked from their landing craft and waded onto the beaches of Da Nang to secure the US airbase in that city. Sixteen days later, on March 24th, the first *teach-in*, a variant of another form of protest, the *sit-in*, was held overnight at the University of Michigan, Ann Arbor where two hundred faculty members held antiwar seminars.

George W. Ball, a man mindful of the French misadventure in Vietnam, served as Under Secretary of State for Economic and Agricultural Affairs for the Johnson and Kennedy administrations. He had told JFK that if combat troops were sent to South Vietnam "within five years we'll have 300,000 men in the paddies and jungles and never find them again."[9] Kennedy had laughed off the estimate saying, "Well, George you're supposed to be one of the smartest guys in town, but you're crazier than hell. That will never happen."[10] Ball later wrote, " [Kennedy's] statement could be interpreted in two ways: either he was convinced that events would so evolve as not to require escalation, or he was determined not to permit such escalation to occur."[11]

US soldiers used derogatory terms such as *gooks, dinks, slants, slopes, charlies,* and *rice-eaters* to describe their foes in Vietnam. Older Vietnamese women were labeled *mamasans,* a word that denotes women who run geisha houses. When US airpower was requested to drop napalm on a location it was referred to as a *barbecue* and enemy combatants who were killed were designated as *wasted.* The North Vietnamese and Viet Cong branded American soldiers as *invaders, imperialists,* and *American bandits.*

On April 7, 1965, in an address at Johns Hopkins University, Johnson reaffirmed his commitment to the fight in South Vietnam: "We will not be defeated. We will not grow tired. We will not withdraw either openly or under the cloak of a meaningless agreement."[12] Ronald Reagan, a California gubernatorial candidate in 1965, thought Johnson could do more to gain a military victory in South Vietnam. Reagan said, "We should declare war on North Vietnam. We could pave the whole country and put parking strips on it and still be home by Christmas."[13]

Echoing Reagan, Air Force General Curtis E. LeMay said, "My solution to the problem would be tell them [the North Vietnamese Communists] frankly that they've got to draw in their horns and stop their aggression or we're going to bomb them back into the Stone Ages."[14] In 1966, Vermont Senator George Aiken came up with a different plan to win the war. Aiken told Johnson to "Declare the United States the winner and begin de-escalation."[15] In 1966 the US had 400,000 soldiers in Vietnam.

Force was only one part of American strategy during the Vietnam War. The people of South Vietnam needed to be won over to support the Saigon government and the process for doing that was referred to as "nation building," a method that included programs with labels such as "new hamlets, "the strategic hamlet program," "civic action," "counterinsurgency," "psychological warfare," "civil operations and revolutionary development support," and "wham"—winning hearts and minds.[16] One term was used extensively. Robert McNamara said in 1966, "*pacification* [is] the main talisman of ultimate US success or failure in Vietnam."[17]

In 1967, Walt W. Rostow, a special assistant to the president for national security affairs, told the press that the *crossover point,* a Vietnamese War term that referred to the level of killed enemy exceeding the number at which the enemy could be replaced, had been reached in Vietnam: "Their casualty rates are going up at a rate they cannot sustain. I see light at the end of the tunnel."[18] That same year, McNamara told Johnson "There may be a limit beyond which Americans and much of the world will not permit the United States to go. The picture of the world's greatest superpower killing or seriously injuring 1,000 noncombatants a week, while trying to pound a tiny, backward nation into submission on an issue whose merits are hotly disputed, is not a pretty one."[19]

South Dakota Senator George McGovern also had concerns about the way America was pursuing the Vietnam War. He said, "We seem bent on saving the Vietnamese from Ho Chi Minh, even if we have to kill them and demolish their country to do it. . . . I do not intend to remain silent in the face of what I regard is a policy of madness, which, sooner or later, will envelope my son and [our] American youth by the millions for years to come."[20] In 1967, the US had 500,000 troops in Vietnam.

In January 1968 the North Vietnamese launched the Tet Offensive, one of the largest military campaigns of the Vietnam War. Although the operation was a military defeat for North Vietnam, it had a profound effect on the US government and shocked the US public, which had been led to believe by its political and military leaders that the North Vietnamese were incapable of launching and sustaining such a comprehensive military action.

During the fighting, on February 7th, American bombs and rockets demolished much of the South Vietnamese city of Ben Tre. Later that day, an American major told Associated Press correspondent Peter Arnett, "it became necessary to destroy the town in order to save it."[21] That quotation, which refers to the decision by allied commanders to bomb and shell Ben Tre regardless of civilian casualties to rout the Viet Cong, morphed into "it became necessary to destroy the village in order to save it."

The testimony given by US Army Lieutenant William L. Calley Jr. during his court martial in 1970-1971 provides another example of the callous brutality of the Vietnam War. Calley, on trial at Fort Benning, Georgia for the premeditated murder of 109 unarmed Vietnamese civilians while on a search-and-destroy mission in the South Vietnamese hamlet of My Lai on March 16, 1968, told prosecutors he had received orders to consider everyone in My Lai as "the enemy."

TV-anchor Walter Cronkite, often cited as "the most trusted man in America" after being so named in an opinion poll, said the following about the Tet Offensive in an editorial at the end of a CBS Evening News broadcast that aired February 17, 1968: "To say that we are mired in stalemate seems the only realistic, yet unsatisfactory, conclusion. . . . it is increasingly clear to this reporter that the only rational way out then will be to negotiate, not as victors, but as an honorable people who lived up to their pledge to defend democracy, and did the best they could."[22] American public support for the war soon declined and the US sought negotiations to end the war. (Marshall McLuhan, commenting on the role the media played in Vietnam, said, "Television brought the brutality of war into the comfort of the living room. Vietnam was lost in the living rooms of America—not on the battlefields of Vietnam."[23])

An indication of public disenchantment with the Vietnam War could be seen in slogans that appeared on protest signs at antiwar rallies: "Hey, Hey, LBJ, How many kids have you killed today?" "Make love, not war," "Drop acid, not bombs," "Draft beer, not boys." There were also antiwar protest songs with titles such as *What Are You Fighting For, Eve of Destruction, I Ain't Marching Anymore,* and *Feel Like I'm Fixin' to Die.* The overarching message of the antiwar protests was that young people in America did not approve of a war their parents' generation wanted them to fight. Idaho Senator Frank Church warned, "This war has already stretched the generation gap so wide that it threatens to pull the country apart."[24]

But the war had its supporters. The conservative group Young Americans for Freedom (YAF) challenged and rebutted antiwar groups like Students for a Democratic Society (SDS) and the War Resisters League (WRL), arguing that everyone should be rooting for a US victory in Vietnam. When President Nixon took office, his vice president, Spiro T. Agnew, denounced opponents of the war, calling them "nattering nabobs of negativity," "an effete corps of impudent snobs," "ideological eunuchs," "professional anarchists," and "vultures who sit in trees."[25] Slogans such as "America, love it or leave it," "My country right or wrong," "No glory like old glory," and "Better dead than red" became rallying cries for champions of the Vietnam War.

Martin Luther King, in a passionate speech delivered in 1967 at Riverside Church in New York City, portrayed the war in Vietnam as an imperial one and said it was "the symptom of a far deeper malady within the American spirit [and that if left untreated would continue to fester and as a result] we shall surely be dragged down the long, dark, and shameful corridors of time reserved for those who possess power and not compassion, might without morality, and strength without sight."[26] Muhammed Ali, who in 1964 had won the WBA, WBC, and lineal heavyweight titles from Sonny Liston, told reporters in Louisville that he would refuse to be inducted into the US military: "Why should they ask me to put on a uniform and go 10,000 miles from home and drop bombs and bullets on brown people in Vietnam after so-called Negro people in Louisville are treated like dogs and denied simple human rights?"[27]

Following the Tet Offensive, pessimism over US prospects in Vietnam deepened among the public and many government officials and advisors. Some in that latter group, a faction known collectively as "The Wise Men," endorsed former Secretary of State Dean Acheson's advice to Johnson, which he gave to the president a couple of weeks after the New Hampshire primary on March 25, 1968: "[with respect to the war in Vietnam] we can no longer do the job we set out to do in the time we have left, and we must begin to take steps to disengage."[28] That remark angered Johnson, who told one of his advisors "You whole group must have been brainwashed."[29] But Johnson, who had barely beaten Eugene McCarthy (a Democrat antiwar candidate) in the New Hampshire primary, saw there was no way to win the Vietnam War and unite his party long enough for him to win re-election in November. On Sunday, March 31st, in a televised speech that pre-empted regular programming, he told the nation "I shall not seek, and I will not accept, the nomination of my party for another term as your President."[30] In 1968, the US had 540,000 soldiers in Vietnam.

On the day after Johnson said he would not run again, Tom Wicker, a political reporter for the *New York Times*, published a column explaining why Johnson was not able to sustain the great mandate that had been conferred upon him in the presidential election of 1964 when he had won 61.1% of the popular vote. Wicker wrote, "The overriding cause for Lyndon Johnson's [electoral] decline from the paths of 1964 and 1965 is the war in Vietnam—too confidently entered upon, too little understood, too costly for any gain he could make men see, too complex either to win or to end by the kind of direct and straightforward action most Americans favor."[31]

Fragging, a word coined by US military personnel during the Vietnam War, is the deliberate killing or attempted killing of a superior officer or non-commissioned officer (NCO) by a fellow soldier; most often with a fragmentation grenade. The large number of *fragging* deaths in the latter stages of the war in Vietnam, along with the high rate of illegal drug use by American soldiers—by 1971 nearly fifty percent of US military serving in Vietnam admitted having "tried" opiate drugs[32]—was indicative of the unpopularity of the Vietnam War within the US military and showed a breakdown of discipline in America's Armed Forces. General Frederick C. Weyand, the last commander of US forces in Vietnam, observed, "When the [American] army is committed, the American people are committed. When the American people lose their commitment, it is futile to try to keep the army committed."[33]

The Nixon Administration

Richard Nixon, who just before the 1968 US presidential election sabotaged President Johnson's attempt to end the Vietnam War by having a surrogate clandestinely tell the South Vietnam government to not meet with their foes,[34] inherited America's military involvement when he became president in 1969. As president, Nixon tried to gain support for a policy of continued military engagement by appealing to the American people "to keep our commitment in Vietnam" and asking the "great silent majority" for their backing as he worked for "peace with honor." Nixon declared, "North Vietnam cannot defeat or humiliate the United States. Only Americans do that."[35] His National Security Advisor, Henry Kissinger, speaking to NSC aides in the autumn of 1969, said, "I refuse to believe that a little fourth-rate power like North Vietnam doesn't have a breaking point."[36] Nixon, like Johnson, said he would not be the "first American President to lose a war."[37]

To make sure he would not be the first American president to lose a war, Nixon, according to his chief of staff H.R. "Bob" Haldeman, came up with an idea that he labeled the *Madman Theory*: "I call it the Madman Theory, Bob. I want the North Vietnamese to believe I've reached the point where I might do anything to stop the war. We'll just slip the word to them that, 'for God's sake, you know Nixon is obsessed about communism. We can't restrain him when he's angry—and he has his hand on the nuclear button and Ho Chi Minh himself will be in Paris in two days begging for peace.'"[38]

Nixon also promoted the idea of *Vietnamization*, a policy meant to end US involvement in Vietnam through a program to "expand, equip and train South Vietnamese forces and assign them to an ever-increasing combat role, at the same time reducing the number of US combat troops."[39] The Vietnamization policy was a response to the Viet Cong's and North Vietnamese Army's Tet Offensive. It referred to US combat troops in their ground combat role but not to fighting by the US Air Force or support of South Vietnam by American military advisors.

The White House Plumbers was a group established during the Nixon presidency to stop the leaking of confidential information to the news media. One leak they didn't stop was the *Pentagon Papers*, a study commissioned by Defense Secretary Robert McNamara that offered a detailed history of the decision-making behind the United States' immersion in Southeast Asia. The *New York Times* published the Papers in a series of blockbuster articles in 1971. They showed the missteps and misrepresentations of four administrations in their Vietnam policies and presented an unremittingly negative view of the possibility of victory in Vietnam.

In a documentary film on the Vietnam War, Daniel Ellsberg, a strategic analyst at the RAND Corporation who released the Pentagon Papers to the *New York Times* and other newspapers, said that America wasn't on the wrong side of the war in Vietnam—we were the wrong side.[40] On April 22, 1971, in testimony before the Senate Foreign Relations Committee, John Kerry (who received several combat medals while serving with the US Navy during the Vietnam War) said, "We saw Vietnam ravaged equally by American bombs as well as by search and destroy missions, as well as by Vietcong terrorism, and yet we listened while this country [the United States] tried to blame all of the havoc on the Vietcong."[41]

The Paris Peace Accords, officially titled the *Agreement on Ending the War and Restoring Peace in Vietnam*, was a peace treaty that included the governments of North Vietnam, South Vietnam, the United States, and the Provisional Revolutionary Government that represented indigenous South Vietnamese revolutionaries. Signed on January 27, 1973, it effectively removed the US from the Vietnam War. For his efforts to end that war, Henry Kissinger won the 1973 Nobel Peace Prize even though a secret bombing campaign he had overseen was still ongoing in Cambodia. Kissinger's award of the Nobel Peace Prize led songwriter Tom Lehrer to quip "[the Norwegian Nobel Committee has] made political satire obsolete."[42]

Conclusion

Saigon fell to the North Vietnamese Army (the NVA) supported by National Liberation Front soldiers (the Viet Cong) on April 30, 1975. That event marked the culmination of the Vietnam War and the start of a transition period to the formal reunification of Vietnam under the Socialist Republic of Vietnam. Commenting on the war's conclusion, in a convocation address that he delivered at Tulane University a week before Saigon was taken over, President Gerald R. Ford (who ascended to the presidency after Nixon resigned in August 1974) said, "Today, America can regain the sense of pride that existed before Vietnam. . . . We of course are saddened by the events in Indochina. But these events, tragic as they are, portend neither the end of the world nor of America's leadership in the world."[43]

After the war the phrase *Vietnam Syndrome* began to be used as a non-medical term that denoted public antipathy for American overseas military involvements. Ronald Reagan, in a speech to a Veterans of Foreign Wars Convention on August 18, 1980, said, "There is a lesson for all of us in Vietnam. If we are forced to fight, we must have the means and determination to prevail or we will not have what it takes to secure the peace."[44] Following the success of Desert Shield/Storm in 1991 (which expelled Iraq from Kuwait), President George H.W. Bush asserted, "It's a proud day for America. And, by God, we've kicked the Vietnam Syndrome once and for all."[45] Bill Clinton's push for a bombing campaign of Yugoslavia in 1999 and the American invasion of Afghanistan in 2001 and Iraq in 2003 offer more evidence that the Vietnam Syndrome has been "kicked."

The Vietnam War was the greatest US military catastrophe of the twentieth century, a disaster that resulted in the loss of more than 58,000 US military personnel, over a trillion inflation-adjusted dollars, and the loss of public trust in America's leaders—and their advisors, a group David Halberstam termed "the best and the brightest" in a book he published in 1972 with that title. It led many to question whether it was a fight the US should have been engaged in. (The US military has estimated that between 200,000-250,000 South Vietnamese soldiers died in the Vietnam War and Hanoi has said that 1.1 million North Vietnamese and Viet Cong fighters and as many as two million North Vietnamese and South Vietnamese civilians also perished. [46])

Language and rhetoric played a large role in getting America into the Vietnam War and language and rhetoric played a similar role in getting America out of it. Language and rhetoric will undoubtedly play a major role in any American military incursion that may be promoted or carried out in the future. Thus, it makes sense to pay close attention to the words employed by government leaders and pundits that encourage US armed engagements abroad. Words have power and, as America's entanglement in Vietnam shows, they can result in significant costs in human lives and treasure and America's standing in the world. Therefore, when it comes to navigating foreign policy and America's relations with other nations to achieve positive outcomes for the United States, it pays for all Americans to use words wisely.

12

What the Fuck: Examining an "Obscene" Term

In 1934, Allen Walker Read, an etymologist, English professor, and good friend of the Institute of General Semantics, published a 15-page, groundbreaking article on taboo language titled "An Obscenity Symbol" in the journal *American Speech*.[1] Due to the linguistic mores of the times, he did not spell out the symbol's name (or use the conventions "the f-word," "f**k," or "f—k"). Instead he alluded to it as "this word," "our word," and "the word that has the deepest stigma of any in the English language." Today he would have simply written "fuck."

"Our word" first appeared in 1528 in a manuscript of the Latin orator Cicero. Reading through the monastery copy of *De Officiis*, an anonymous monk wrote in the margin of the text "O d fuckin Abbot."[2] It is not known whether "fuckin" referred to the abbot having sex or was an intensifier, but the cleric was careful not to write the word "damned," which is what the letter "d" stood for—in the 16th century blasphemy trumped sexual allusions with respect to what was considered truly obscene.

In 1598, John Florio published *A Worlde of Wordes*, an Italian-English dictionary whose aim was to define words in Italian and English as they were actually spoken. It is full of *fucks*—*fottere* is defined as "to jape, to sard, to fuck, to swive, to occupy," *fortice* includes the terms "a woman fucker and a swiver," and *fottitore* is the male counterpart of *fortice*. While *fuck* appeared in print in the 16th century, it was used in common speech before then.

In 1671, *fuck* was given a dictionary entry in its proper alphabetic place by Thomas Henshaw's *Etymologicon Linguae Anglicanae*. *Fuck* also appeared in Nathaniel Bailey's *Universal Etymological English Dictionary* (1721) and John Ash's *New and Complete Dictionary of the English Language* (1775). Samuel Johnson omitted *fuck* from his highly influential *Dictionary of the English Language* (1755)—Johnson would not allow the inclusion of any language he could not repeat in genteel society.

Many of the new dictionaries in the middle and latter parts of the 18th century were produced for use in schools, and *fuck* was omitted from them over concerns of corrupting young minds. In the 19th century, Johnson's omission of the word in his dictionary set the tone for dictionary writers such as Noah Webster (who excluded *fuck* in his dictionaries of 1806, 1807, 1817, 1828, and 1841) and Sir James Murray (editor of the *Oxford English Dictionary* who, in 1898, omitted *fuck* in the *OED*). The 1873 Comstock Act, which prohibited the mailing of "obscene," "lewd," or "lascivious" material, also limited the use of *fuck* in print.

The copious use of *fuck* by soldiers during WWI made it possible for the word to return to the printed page (swearing was commonplace for doughboys, as their seclusion from polite society meant there was no one about to censure them from speaking this way). After the war, *fuck* appeared in *Ulysses* (1922) and *Lady Chatterley's Lover* (1928), which caused those books to be frequently banned and confiscated by government authorities—in 1933, the US Postal Service ruled *Ulysses* could be sent through the mail. The courts did not clear *Lady Chatterley's Lover* until 1959 in the United States and 1960 in England.

From privates to generals, *fuck* was used by millions of men in uniform during World War II. It served as a stand-in while thinking of a more suitable word, but it was more often employed as an expletive. *Fuck's* copious use during the war led it to lose some of its stigma but among some civilians it still remained a taboo word. In 1948, when Norman Mailer published *The Naked and the Dead*, a gritty novel that depicts the experiences of a platoon during World War II, he was forced to substitute the word *fug* for *fuck*. In the 1957 musical *West Side Story*, Stephen Sondheim opted for "buggin'" (the Jets want to best "Every last buggin' gang on the whole buggin' street") and the lyric "Gee, Officer Krupke, krup you!"

In the 1950s and 1960s, *fuck* was frequently printed as is in mainstream fiction and nonfiction. James Jones used it fifty times in his 1951 National Book Award winning novel *From Here to Eternity* and J.D. Salinger utilized it in *Catcher in the Rye (*1951). John O'Hara in *Ten North Frederick* (1955), Allen Ginsberg in his poem *Howl* (1956), and many other writers also incorporated the term in their manuscripts.

The protest era of the 1960s led to greater usage and acceptance of the word. It was uttered once in the film *Vapor* (1965) and in two Andy Warhol films—*Poor Little Rich Girl* (1965) and *My Hustler* (1965). In 1970, Robert Altman's R-rated black comedy M*A*S*H became the first major film to use *fuck*. (The MPAA rating system assigns a PG-13 rating now if a film contains the word once. The R rating is normally required if the film contains two utterances of the word or if the word is used in a sexual context.)

An important victory for breaking the taboo around *fuck* came in *Cohen v. California* (1971); a Supreme Court case that involved a Vietnam War protestor who in the public corridors of a California courthouse wore a jacket bearing the phrase "Fuck the Draft." The court ruled that the protestor could not be criminally prosecuted for a public display of the word *fuck*, as it did not fall into other categories of proscribed speech such as *fighting words* or *obscenity*.

Shortly thereafter the Supreme Court, in the case of *FCC v. Pacifica Foundation* (1978), created a category of lesser-protected speech for the term *fuck*: *indecency*. The case involved the airing on radio of comedian George Carlin's now infamous monologue *Seven Words You Can Never Say on Television*, which included *fuck* and *motherfucker*. The FCC said it could weigh in on the action based on upon its statutory authority to restrict "any obscene, indecent, or profane language." The Supreme Court agreed with the FCC, ruling the agency could impose administrative sanctions on broadcasters that allowed the transmission of offensive language that was indecent.

The use of the word *fuck* increased in the 1980s and 1990s. In 1998, the *New York Times* printed the word in full, as part of their commitment to publishing the Starr Report: "Ms. Lewinsky said she wanted two things from the President. The first was contrition: He needed to 'acknowledge' . . . that he helped fuck up my life."[3]

Fuck is not that widely used in politics and its use sometimes promotes controversy. Some examples of its use in the political arena include the following: In June 2004, Vice President Cheney told Democratic Senator Patrick Leahy, "Go fuck yourself." On March 23, 2010, Vice President Joe Biden, referring to the US health care reform bill, whispered to President Barack Obama that "This is a big fucking deal." In 2021, "Let's go Brandon" became a political slogan and internet meme as a euphemism for "Fuck Joe Biden."

Fuck's appearance in music goes back a bit. Louise Brogan's "dirty blues" recording of *Shave 'Em Dry* (1935) made use of the word, with lyrics such as "I fucked all night / And the night before, baby/ And I feel like I wanna fuck some more," which gave some insight into what was actually being sung in clubs at the time. Today's use of *fuck* in music is ubiquitous, particularly with hip-hop and heavy metal groups—song titles with the word *fuck* in them include *Fuck the Police* by N.W.A, *Nazi Punks Fuck Off* by Dead Kennedys, and *Fuck the Pain Away* by Peaches.

Fuck has become a versatile word that can be grammatically employed as a:

Verb—They fuck all the time.

Noun—You're such a fuck.

Pronoun—Hey, fuck-face.

Adverb—He fucking screamed as loud as he could.

Conjunction—I went swimming; fuck the cold (as in, I went swimming despite the cold).

Interjection—Fuck! I hit my elbow.

Fuck also has a wide variety of meanings:

Aggression—Fuck you!

Apathy—Who gives a fuck.

Confusion—What the fuck?

Despair— Fucked again.

Fraud—I got fucked.

Greetings—How the fuck are you?

Ignorance—How the fuck do I know?

Incompetence—He's a fuckup.

Laziness—He's a fuckoff.

Wonder—How the fuck did you do that?

And *fuck* is a component of many acronyms:

SNAFU—Situation Normal: All Fucked Up

FUBAR—Fucked Up Beyond All Recognition

WTF—What the Fuck

STFU—Shut the Fuck Up

BAMF—Badass Motherfucker

OMFG—Oh My Fucking God

Fuck is clearly a resilient word, but its saturation and overuse is probably diminishing its offensiveness—to quote the linguist Ruth Wajnryb: ". . . nowadays it takes more FUCK's to achieve what one lone FUCK would have achieved ten years ago."[4] Richard Dooling, the author of *Blue Streak: Swearing, Free Speech, and Sexual Harassment,* notes that *fuck* has lost its position as the king of offensive terms: "[f]or centuries, *fuck* was the most objectionable word in the English language, but now *nigger* and *cunt* are probably tied for that distinction, and fuck has at long last stepped down."[5]

Allen Walker Read, writing about why *fuck* was considered so obscene and carried such a great stigma, argued it was partly because of the "fearful thrill" it gave to people from "seeing, doing, or speaking the forbidden."[6] As the use of the word has become more prevalent in society that "fearful thrill" and *fuck's* status as a major obscenity has lessened. This is understandable, as the shelf life of words considered profane typically diminishes over time—*damn* and *hell* were the worst obscenities in the 16th century. Today, as the linguist John McWhorter notes, "They are hardly the kind of words that leave you looking around to see if anyone else heard."[7]

George Carlin's take on profanity was that "These words have no power. We give them power by refusing to be free and easy with them. We give them power over us. They really, in themselves, have no power."[8] A general semanticist might say, the meaning of words is not in words—it's in people.

Fuck's meaning has morphed quite a bit since Allen Walker Read wrote about "our word" in 1934. It is no longer "the word that has the deepest stigma of any in the English language." *Fuck* has become an equal opportunity pejorative for those who care to use it.

Allen Walker Read felt he could not write *fuck* in his scholarly article discussing that word. This constraint no longer holds, as is evidenced by the chapter you are now reading, a treatise that underscores the general semantics notion, *the only thing permanent in life is change.*

Indexing the American Revolutionary War

The American Revolutionary War is classically depicted as a war between the "Americans" and the British. That is only part of the story, and it presumes an actual national identity. It was also a war between Patriots (supporters of independence) and Loyalists (backers of King George), Patriots and Native Americans, Britain and other nations in the world, and African Americans and those they thought would be less likely to grant them freedom. These "wars" will be explored in this chapter using *indexing,* a general semantics device that employs subscript numbers attached to broad terms. The purpose of indexing is to help people to detect important and meaningful differences in the word being indexed.[1]

Indexing the American Revolutionary War

The Revolutionary War$_1$: Patriots versus Loyalists

There is no way of ascertaining with any degree of certainty how many "Americans" were for breaking away from Britain, were loyal to King George, or were fence sitters. Current thought indicates about 20 percent of the colonists stayed loyal to Britain and the King, 40-55 percent of the white population supported the Patriots' cause, and the rest were neutral.

Loyalists (*aka* King's Men, Tories, and Royalists) thought themselves British citizens and consequently believed the Revolution to be treason. Many Loyalists were older, more established, and members of the merchant class whose livelihoods hung on good relations with Britain. Many were concerned that disruption and mob rule might ensue from a revolution. Some were hopeful that independence from Britain would eventually come, but like many of America's Founding Fathers who opposed slavery but did not resist its inclusion in the US Constitution, they thought change would happen slowly.

A number of prominent Loyalists believed there was lots of support among the colonists for England and conveyed that idea to the British. However, this turned out not to be true and British reliance on a belief that large numbers of Loyalists would fight with them worked to their detriment in terms of military planning.

Families were often divided during the American Revolution. Benjamin Franklin's son William, the last Colonial Governor of New Jersey (1763-1776), was a staunch Loyalist throughout the Revolutionary War, organizing military units to fight with the British—he coordinated a group known as the *Associated Loyalists* that waged guerilla warfare in New York, New Jersey and Connecticut. After the war, William went into exile in Britain, living in London until his death. (Benjamin Franklin, a reluctant but energetic patriot, was not happy with his son's decision to side with the British. In his will he left his son nothing except title to land he no longer owned in Nova Scotia.)

General Benedict Arnold was one of the most famous Loyalists. Other well-known Loyalists include the governor of the Massachusetts Bay Colony, Thomas Hutchinson; the Pennsylvania delegate to the First Continental Congress, Joseph Galloway; and the mayor of New York City, David Mathews.

Patriots were opposed to people with Loyalist inclinations, and before and during the Revolution there were numerous instances of Loyalists being beaten, tarred and feathered, and having their property destroyed. Thomas Paine defined a Loyalist as a person "apostate from the order of manhood." For their part, the Loyalists believed they were the ethical and more noble group, and the Patriots were like petulant, unreasoning children held captive by their emotions.

Over 20,000 Tories fought against their rebel neighbors during the Revolutionary War, and some battles, such as the Battle of Ramsour's Mill, which occurred on June 20, 1780 in what is now Lincolnton, North Carolina, were wholly American v American affairs. At the Battle of Kings Mountain, which took place in what is now rural Cherokee County, South Carolina on October 7, 1780, British Major Patrick Ferguson commanded a group of 900 Loyalist troops. An elite provincial regiment known as the British Legion that was composed of Loyalists and a detachment of English Light Dragoons was particularly feared and hated for its savagery and reputation for executing prisoners.

When the Revolutionary War ended, approximately 100,000 Tories emigrated to British North America (now Canada), between 80,000 to 100,000 fled to the West Indies, around 5,000 Southern Loyalists moved to Florida, and roughly 7,000 to 8,000 Loyalists went to Great Britain. The Paris Peace Treaty (1783) contained provisions requiring a stop to the seizure of Loyalist property and Loyalists staying in America were generally able to retain their property and become US citizens. Some Loyalists who stayed recovered their neighbors' goodwill while others became outcasts.

American history brands Loyalists as "traitors." But most were just trying to keep lifestyles to which they had become accustomed. Had the British won the war, Washington, Adams, and Jefferson would have been the traitors. But the winners write history, so Washington, Adams, Jefferson, and America's other Founding Fathers, are labeled heroes. To the victors belong the (linguistic) spoils.

The Revolutionary War$_2$: Patriots versus Native Americans

In the 18th century, the growing British colonial population had concerns about Native Americans, who felt less pressure from the French colonists, as they were fewer in numbers. The French understood this, and tried to win Indigenous people to their side. The British countered, by offering higher-quality trade goods at lower prices than the French. The Indians played on British-French rivalry to get from each side whatever advantage they could.

The French-Indian War (1754-1763) matched the colonies of British America against those of New France, each group assisted by military units from the parent country and by Indian allies. The British colonists were helped at various times by the Iroquois, Catawba, and Cherokee tribes. The French colonists were supported by the Abenaki, Micmac, Algonquin, Lenape, Ojibwa, Ottawa, Shawnee, and Wyandot tribes. The war ended with the Paris Treaty of 1763, which provided the British with huge territorial gains.

During the Revolutionary War, many Indians fought with the British, as they believed American independence would hasten their dispossession and enslavement. Among this group were the Mohawk, Seneca, Cayuga, and Onondaga tribes. In the Southeast, the Cherokee split into a pro-Patriot faction and a pro-British faction that the Americans referred to as the Chickamauga Cherokee. Other tribes were also divided.

In the West, where Indians were more numerous, the Patriots tried to secure Indian neutrality. Most Indigenous chiefs initially accepted neutrality as their best option, not wanting to endanger Indian lives and land by backing what could be an eventual loser.

In July 1776, a militant faction of Cherokees, tired of having settlers invade their terrain, attacked settlements in the western counties of North and South Carolina. Patriots claimed the Indians acted on behalf of the British and used that claim to garner the support of the settlers, which resulted in 6,000 settler-militiamen attacking and destroying several Cherokee villages.

Many Indians regarded the British as the lesser of two evils, seeing them as calculating allies who were not averse to spilling Indian blood. Tribes that allied with the British received rum, guns, ammunition, clothing, hatchets, hoes, mirrors, and jewelry. Indian support for the British was largely transactional, increasing when the British won battles, decreasing after defeats. Some tribes shifted their alliance from one side to the other.

In February 1779, Congress authorized a punitive mission into "Indian country." The campaign against the Iroquois Confederacy involved over one-third of the Continental army and was directly supervised and planned by George Washington, who ordered the eradication of the enemy's crops—today this would be labeled a form of genocide. Fortunately for the Indians, Washington's large and slow-moving army was easily seen and so it was easy to retreat. But the Indians' entire housing stock was destroyed along with many of their horses, cows, and pigs.

When the British made peace with the Americans in the Treaty of Paris (1783), Indians were not mentioned in its terms, which involved the cession of huge amounts of Indian land to the United States—the cession doubled the size of the new nation. The Indians had mostly sided with the British and in the minds of the Patriots this meant they had given up the rights to their land.

The Revolutionary War$_3$: African-Americans versus the Patriots and the British

Of the roughly half million enslaved people living in the colonies at the start of the Revolutionary War, perhaps twenty thousand fought for or against the British. Most stayed on their farms and plantations because they feared execution if captured by the Patriots and worried about revenge on their families and friends. Some fled to the countryside or sought sanctuary by trudging along with the British army.

In April 1775, Lord Dunmore, a Scottish Peer and Virginia's Royal Governor, threatened to free slaves and burn down Williamsburg, the capital of Virginia, if the colonists rebelled against British authority. Seven months later he issued a proclamation that established martial law and offered freedom to slaves who would leave Patriot owners and join with the British. Within a month, 300 slaves signed up with Dunmore's "Royal Ethiopian Regiment" and 500 more soon followed. Dunmore's proclamation motivated thousands of slaves during the Revolutionary War to seek liberty behind British lines.

Many British commanders used runaway slaves as laborers and foragers. But mostly, the British were ambivalent about what to do with slaves. That uncertainty cost them, as training runaway Black troops for combat might have helped the British win the war in the South. The few Blacks they did arm incensed southern whites, who became willing consumers of Patriot propaganda linking the British with slaves, outlaws, and Indians.

When the war began, there was a lack of white male volunteers signing up for service in the Continental Army. This led a number of states to entertain the idea of recruiting Black men willing to fight for their freedom. Accordingly, in 1775, the New England states enlisted 200 Blacks. But George Washington favored a popular notion that Blacks were too cowardly to fight and that training them would threaten white domination, so he ceased their procurement. In January 1778, Washington reversed himself and endorsed plans by the New England states to recruit slaves by promising them eventual freedom, and compensating their masters.

In May 1779, Congress approved a scheme that recommended South Carolina and Georgia arm 3,000 slaves, who would receive no pay but be given $50 and their freedom if they survived the war. Congress said it would compensate slaveholders for any of their slaves who enlisted. The South Carolina legislature nixed the idea and instead tried to recruit more white men by promising each a bounty that included a slave paid for by the state.

Virginia contemplated recruiting Black soldiers in late 1780. But, like South Carolina, Virginia legislators demurred. Instead they offered each white recruit a slave and 100 acres of land. Despite the new incentives, few whites enlisted to satisfy Virginia's quota to the Continental Army and when drafted to serve, some white men sent slaves as substitutes, promising them their freedom if they lived through the war.

Most Black soldiers in the Continental Army served in integrated regiments where they worked as wagon drivers, cooks, waiters, and in other support roles. Several all-Black units, commanded by white officers, were formed and fought against the British. Blacks also served as sailors on privateers and in the Continental Navy. Many more Black men served in the North, as opposed to the South, because of deep racial bias in the South.

Many Northern states eliminated slavery after the war (Vermont was the first new state to join the Union slavery). In some of those states, Blacks were given the franchise for a limited time. But the Constitution preserved slavery, and it would not be abolished until after the Civil War, more than seventy-five years later.

The Revolutionary War₄: France, Spain, and the Dutch Republic versus Britain

British victory over the French in the French and Indian War (1754-1763)was part of a global conflict known as the Seven Years War (1756-1763) wherein France lost almost all its New World possessions. The French only managed to retain a few small islands off the coast of Canada and in the Caribbean.

Spain entered the Seven Years War as an ally of France in 1761. The war went badly for the Spanish, with Britain seizing Manila and Havana from them. To get those places back, Spain was forced to cede Florida to the British. France compensated Spain for its losses in the war by ceding Louisiana west of the Mississippi (along with New Orleans) to Spain.

With the outbreak of the American Revolution in 1775, France and Spain saw possibilities to capitalize on the conflict. France hoped to replace Britain as America's largest trading partner and Spain wanted to regain lost territory.

In the early years of the war, France and Spain assisted the colonists covertly, smuggling money, gunpowder, and supplies to the insurrectionists. In December 1776, King Carlos III of Spain issued a royal order to the governors of Louisiana and Cuba to open Spanish ports in the New World to American merchant vessels. In October 1777, the Americans defeated the British at Saratoga. That victory convinced the French that America could effectively fight the British and led, in February 1778, to France and the United States signing a treaty of alliance that stipulated American independence as a condition of peace.

After the French entered the war, Spain offered the use of Spanish ports along the northern coast of Spain to American privateers, which allowed those ships to swap their buccaneer booty for military supplies to help the war effort. In April 1779, Spain signed a mutual military alliance with France that stipulated the French would help in the capture of Gibraltar, Minorca, and Florida and, in return, Spain would aid France in the war with Britain. France and Spain agreed that Spanish forces would only attack British possessions outside the United States, as Spain, a major colonial powers, did not want to be seen as directly aiding a colony in revolt.

The Dutch also supported the American cause. Dutch merchants, as early as 1774, provided gunpowder and supplies to the American revolutionaries, much of it sent from St. Eustatius, a Dutch run island in the Caribbean. This did not make the British happy and, as Dutch merchants continued to trade with France and the United States, they declared war on the Dutch Republic in 1780. As payback, on April 19, 1782, The Republic of the United Netherlands became the second nation after France to recognize America as an independent country. Spain recognized America on February 20, 1783, seven months before Great Britain.

French maritime and land forces were essential to the defeat of Cornwallis at Yorktown. Being victorious in the Revolutionary War was particularly important for the prestige and pride of France. (Unfortunately for Louis XVI, the costs of supporting the American Revolution were a contributing factor to the overthrow of the government of France and his execution in 1793 during the French Revolution.)

Though the Revolutionary War cost Britain its colonies in America, the British retained Canada and land in the Caribbean, Africa, and India. Britain would later expand in those regions, building what has been termed the "Second British Empire," which eventually became the largest empire in the history of the world. From a global perspective, the aftermath of the American Revolution was not a lethal blow to Britain, as Britain became the world's hegemon for more than a hundred years.

PART V

Three GS Satires

Beware High Level Abstractions

Yesterday I had lunch with the American people. I had wanted to speak with them for the longest time, as they are a highly influential group of folks often mentioned by politicians on TV news programs.

I met the people at a diner near where I live. I ordered a BLT with coleslaw on the side and a cup of coffee. The people ordered cheeseburger specials with double fries and Diet Cokes. I told the waitress to give everyone separate checks.

After some idle chitchat about the huge portions of food typically served in diners, I asked the American people to tell me their thoughts on wearing masks and getting vaccinated to prevent Covid. They started to answer the question before I could finish it and the cacophony and contempt that individuals within the group had for those who did not share their views was just crazy. Luckily, I had a whistle in my pocket and after blowing it as loud as I could the crowd calmed down. It turned out 30% of the people thought mask wearing and taking shots to prevent Covid was a bad idea, 50% thought it was a good idea, 10% said it was a good idea on weekdays but a bad one on weekends, 7 percent had no opinion on the matter, and 3% said the pandemic was fake news. I moved on to illegal immigration.

"Do you think a security fence should be built on the Mexican border? Do you support a guest worker program? Are you in favor of granting amnesty to undocumented individuals currently living in the United States?"

The people popped right in with answers, which they argued about forcefully with each other, some waving knives and forks in their hands. I worried it might get physical so, after again blowing hard on my whistle, I told everyone to calm down and give a little thought to what they were saying. I was advised that's not how American's roll. One guy said, "We are not a nation of deliberators. We know what we think and want to express our views quickly so we don't get confused in case someone interrupts us with different ideas."

I pleaded with the people to keep their voices down, warning if they didn't we might be asked to leave. My plea worked, and was helped by having our food brought out from the kitchen. As the plates were being set down, the people began to argue about who should sit where. I said I didn't think it mattered where anyone sat and while they were debating the issue their food was getting cold. No one seemed to care about that and the squabbling continued so I took out my trusty whistle, gave it a blow, and said, "How about we stop the bickering and just enjoy the meal," to which I was told "Mind your own business and pass the salt."

I had wanted to talk to the people about the economy, race relations, abortion, and a host of other topics but I didn't have the strength to keep blowing my whistle. That a third of the American people were packing guns also made me wary to mention anything that was controversial. So I decided to talk about something I thought was innocuous. "Nice weather we're having," I said to my tablemates.

Meteorology was not the conversational safe harbor I thought it would be. Some of the people said the weather did not look nice to them, others accused me of being a climate-change denier, and a few demanded to know why I was talking about the weather when there were so many more interesting and important subjects we could talk about. Rather than respond to their remarks I asked for the checks.

The checks totaled two billion dollars, minus the tips; not a bad price for three hundred thirty million cheeseburger specials. The bad part was the only thing everyone agreed on was that I should pay for the food. I didn't want to fight such a petulant throng so

I agreed to pick up the tab, which didn't make me happy, as the limit on my credit card is ten thousand dollars.

I asked the waitress if I could pay with a personal check. She said I could as long as I had a form of photo ID. Fortunately, I did.

As I got into my car to go home two thoughts struck me. The next time I speak to the American people I will do it on social media platforms, where you don't have to feed folks to get them to talk and you can be as outlandish, unthinking, and arbitrary as you like; and after my check bounces, I doubt if I will ever be welcomed to eat at this diner again.

Words, Meanings and People

The *Diagnostic and Statistical Manual of Mental Disorders* (*DSM*) is a guidebook used by mental health professionals to diagnose and classify mental disorders. Among the disorders not currently listed in the DSM are the following four conditions that in my opinion are worthy of consideration.

Paying Attention Disorder (PAD)

Paying Attention Disorder is a psychological condition that involves being attentive to whomever or whatever one is involved with. It can be seen in individuals who try to engage others in meaningful discussion rather than speak on their cell phones, text, or tweet during conversations. These people genuinely attempt to talk and listen to the individuals around them. Typically, their efforts are ignored because paying attention to others during person-to-person exchanges is a useless artifact from the pre-internet era.

To overcome PAD, the patient should watch TV talk shows and listen to political debates. Working for a telecommunications company is also recommended, as telecom employees are specially trained to never pay attention to anyone. Alternatively, the patient can try to find employment as a customer-relations representative for a cable company or major American airline.

Single Personality Disorder (SPD)

To meet the ongoing challenges and changing conditions that characterize today's hectic, fast-paced world, one must be pliant and be able to reinvent oneself. That's a lot easier to do if you have multiple personalities. If you have just one it's almost impossible.

Imagine you are a shy, humorless person with a single personality who is working as a reference librarian and the library you work for shuts down. You've got bills to pay and you need to find a job quickly but the only employment available in town is doing standup at Sam's Cabaret and Comedy Club. Sadly, you won't make much money if Sam hires you because reciting numbers from the Dewey Decimal System isn't very funny.

To gain additional personalities, the patient should be encouraged to watch movies and adopt the personas of the various characters appearing on the screen. Another strategy the patient can use is to ask a person with multiple personalities if he or she would be willing to sell a few of them. Finally, the patient can buy a lotto ticket and hope they win the grand prize. If that happens the patient can behave however they want.

Lack of Narcissism Personality Disorder (LNPD)

"Narcissistic personality disorder" is listed as a mental condition in the *DSM*. But this categorization is no longer valid, as recent studies indicate that those who have an exaggerated sense of their own importance are the rule in American society. The problem is lack of narcissism, which, to put a label on it, could be classified as Lack of Narcissism Personality Disorder (LNPD).

To treat LNPD, advise the patient to go to Bloomingdale's with a credit card and say to the salespeople there, "I want to look better than everyone else on the planet. Can you help me to do that?" The *oohs* and *ahs* that the patient will receive from the fawning sales staff as they buy loads of expensive clothing and accouterments should convince them that they're the cat's meow. Coaching on how to dominate conversations and dump blame on others when you make a mistake are useful adjuncts in developing an outsized sense of self-importance.

Talk Radio Addiction (TRA)

Talk Radio Addiction is a compulsion to listen to talk radio programs and then accuse one's spouse and colleagues of being wacky out-of-touch liberals who should leave the country if they think things are so bad. TRA sufferers are fond of conflict and refuse to be swayed by the facts. When they take a stand on something they will normally brook no opposition, however a rant by Sean Hannity or a radical lobotomy may occasionally lead them to reverse an opinion.

TRA is a difficult disease to treat because the patient does not think he is sick. He thinks you are. Diverting the patient's attention can be tried and while he is distracted one can switch the channel to a sports or music station. Over time the patient may develop a liking for one of those forms of entertainment. In some cases, surgery has been successful in opening a person's mind but the procedure is risky and should only be attempted by highly trained specialists who have tremendous patience in dealing with complete and total morons.

Semantic Antics

From the Boston Tea Party to the insurrection at the US Capitol in 2021, Americans have always been partisan and headstrong. Some have explained this by saying that it is in our genes and cultural DNA to act that way and TV and social media have made the problem worse. But I believe the explanation for why Americans are opinionated and temperamental is simpler than that: it's English, with its histrionic parts of speech that lead us to rancor and division. Case in point, proper nouns.

Proper nouns, because they are spelled with initial capital letters, think they are better than all the other nouns, which they label as common. The "common" nouns understandably hate that tag and try to get back at the proper nouns wherever and whenever they can. When proper nouns are used in a sentence the common ones will often mock them as being condescending, snobbish, stick-in-the-muds. Sometimes they will put a banana peel in the middle of a sentence just to see if they can get a proper noun to slip on it and cause the sentence to fragment.

Possessive nouns are nouns that claim proprietorship over other words, using apostrophes to get the job done (e.g., the cat's toy, John's book, Betty's land). When different grammatical constructions are used instead of them (e.g., the toy the cat has, the book John owns, the land Betty possesses) they will often become distressed and throw hissy fits. Possessive nouns are no fun to be with at parties because when anyone speaks about anything they will assert ownership over the topic being discussed.

Reflexive pronouns (himself, herself, myself, etc.) are not *pro* nouns. Rather, they are pro themselves and reflexively don't care about any other parts of speech. Reflexive pronouns think they are the hottest things going. Instead of quietly and thoughtfully functioning by their lonesome as noun phrases, these jokers get their jollies by letting every word within linguistic hailing distance know it's all about them. When having discussions, they typically talk only about themselves—or any of the other words ending in self or selves.

Let's look at verbs. When an action verb is transitive it is followed by a direct object, for example, "let's eat pie." When an action verb is intransitive, it does not have a direct object, to wit, "let's eat." Each of these verb classes thinks their way of handling objects is the correct one. Because of that conviction, when transitive verbs and intransitive verbs get thrown together in the same paragraph there's often hell to pay and interjections such as "Yipes!" or "What!" get bandied about.

Speaking of interjections, these utterances invariably piss off all the other syntactical categories, as they are viewed by other words as being superfluous to the meaning of a sentence and the exclamation points that frequently follow them are seen as arrogant. That the rules of English allow interjections to be used as standalone sentences is another reason they are disliked.

Adjectives, adverbs, and prepositions are despised by nouns and verbs that resent being modified; conjunctions are hated for making sentences longer than they should be; and articles are pooh-poohed for being small in number and having to sidle up to nouns to make their presence felt. Long story short, the components of English are crazy and that the language has not been institutionalized can only be ascribed to luck or the fact that if you locked up all its grammatical parts we would have nothing to say because we would not have the means to say it.

So the next time you are in a situation where someone is spouting political talking points in a venomous and hysterical manner, don't get all lathered up about it. It's not that they are biased, low-information dumbbells who have rocks in their heads and know squat about politics. It's English that's making them talk like fools.

PART VI

Three GS Poems

Is Everybody Happy?

There is no algorithm for happiness
but I ask Siri anyway. She replies,
*surveys say Switzerland is the happiest
country in the world, not sure why, could
be the chocolate, maybe it's the cheese.*

Buddhists say to attain contentment
one must overcome cravings for
iPhones, Patek Philippe watches, BMWs,
and early bird dinners served till six.

Scientists have the ability to
measure happiness but not as
well as novelists, poets, and my
ninety-five-year-old mother.

Happiness is the only thing
humans desire for its own sake,
said Aristotle, to which Thoreau
replied: joy is like a butterfly,
the more you chase it, the more
it will elude you.

For Linus, happiness is a
warm blanket. For me,
it's a toasted bagel with
peanut butter, jelly,
cup of coffee on the side.

Labels

I am a jigsaw puzzle with bent and
broken pieces that if dropped in a

therapist's office would scatter its
social construction and fall into a

multicultural mélange that emerged
about 200,000 years ago in East Africa

and spread through Eurasia, Oceania, and
the Americas, feeding and interbreeding,

speaking thousands of different languages,
framing the world in ways Charles Darwin

and Walt Whitman would say are both
unique and commonplace and not easily

categorized by checking a box on a
census form.

Ode to the Structural Differential

I hail Alfred Korzybski's physical model
of reality in which a disc and suitcase-
shaped tags show that I abstract from
my environments, that there is a
sub-atomic domain beyond my
direct observation, that what
I experience I cannot fully
describe, and that there
is more to heaven
and earth than
is contained
in my verbal philosophy.

Coda

A Brief History of the Institute
of General Semantics

In 1933, Alfred Korzybski published his second book, *Science and Sanity: An Introduction to Non-Aristotelian Systems and General Semantics*, twelve years after his first, *Manhood of Humanity: The Science and Art of Human Engineering*.

Science and Sanity created a major stir among scholars and intellectuals, and in 1934 Korzybski began traveling around America to promote his work, which he referred to as *general semantics*. Between January 1935 and the first seminar offered by the Institute in July 1938, Korzybski delivered seminars or lectures at twelve colleges and universities (University of Kansas, Washington State Normal School, University of Washington, Williams Institute in Berkeley, University of Michigan, Olivet College, the Wistar Institute in Philadelphia, the Galois Institute of Mathematics at Long Island University, Columbia University, Northwestern University, the University of Chicago, and Harvard University); three hospitals (the Menninger Clinic in Topeka, Kansas, New Jersey's Marlboro State Hospital, and Peoria State Hospital); and at conferences and privately-organized seminars in St. Louis and in Los Angeles.

Korzybski sought to educate his readers and students on how to evaluate and respond more effectively to the diverse experiences they encountered in life, particularly with respect to properly reacting and adjusting to symbolic stimuli, such as language. He theorized that much, if not most, of human anguish could be traced to pre-scientific misevaluations of the way we function as the only form of time-binding symbol users.

The Institute of General Semantics was incorporated in Chicago because that is where Douglas Gordon Campbell and Charles B. Congdon, psychiatrists at the Student Health Service of the University of Chicago, lived and worked. They were both very interested in Korzybski's system and wanted him to come there. Through Dr. Campbell, Cornelius Crane (heir to Crane Plumbing) also became involved and contributed $25,000 to the initial funding of the Institute. The Institute's incorporating certificate listed Korzybski, Campbell, Congdon, and Crane as the four trustees. Additionally, Marjory [*sic*] Kendig was listed as an ex-officio member of the Board.

In the 1930s, new ground was being broken in many academic fields and leaders in various disciplines, many of whom Korzybski corresponded with in the process of writing *Science and Sanity,* were invited to become Honorary Trustees of the Institute. A long list of eminent scholars accepted—there were a total of thirty-one Honorary Trustees at the Institute's inception.

With a beginning funding, and strong financial backing, the new Institute was launched in May 1938, with an office in a small apartment two blocks from the University of Chicago. Two months later the new Institute presented its first seminar (it consisted of twelve lectures delivered by Korzybski on Monday and Wednesday evenings over a six-week period). In 1939, the Institute moved one block west to a house with the numerically intriguing address 1234 E. 56th Street.

Many of the future leaders of the nascent discipline of general semantics came to Korzybski's early seminars, men such as Elwood Murray, Irving J. Lee, S. I. Hayakawa, Francis Chisholm, Wendell

Johnson, Ray Bontrager, and Dr. Douglas Kelley. Other individuals who have taken Institute seminars, lectures, or workshops include the novelist, short story writer, essayist, painter, and spoken work performer William S. Burroughs; inventor, architect, philosopher, writer, etc. R. Buckminster Fuller; science-fiction writer Robert Heinlein; psychologist and author Abraham Maslow; British physician and co-author with John Cleese of *Families: And How to Survive Them* Robin Skynner; contemporary science-fiction writer Robert Anton Wilson; and author, entertainer, and composer Steve Allen.

In 1939, Hitler's armies invaded Poland and Belgium. In 1940, France fell, and London was being blitzed from the air. Korzybski noted the impact that some of these disasters had on him in his Introduction to the second edition of *Science and Sanity*, which was published in 1941, the year the Japanese attacked Pearl Harbor.

A number of students who had attended Institute seminars joined America's armed forces during World War II and some took *Science and Sanity* with them to their combat postings. In Army hospitals in Europe, Dr. Douglas Kelley used Korzybskian methods to help treat soldiers suffering from battle fatigue and fear.

In the midst of the hostilities raging in Europe, the IGS held a Second American Congress on General Semantics (the first took place in 1935 at The Washington Normal School in Ellensburg, Washington) at the University of Denver in August 1941. It was well attended, with many fine papers published in 1943 in the volume *Papers from the Second American Congress on General Semantics* (M. Kendig, Editor).

Korzybski presented a number of seminars in Chicago, about six each year, as well as some in California, New York City, and elsewhere. But revenues earned from these endeavors were barely able to keep the IGS afloat. Fortunately, Mrs. Frances Stone

Dewing, the mother of Mary Morain (a social reformer and leading secular humanist who compiled and edited four books on general semantics), provided generous financial help at this critical juncture. In 1942, a small group of Korzybski's students in Chicago got together to establish the Society for General Semantics, an organization whose aim was to interest the public in GS and put out a general semantics journal. Five dollars of their annual ten-dollar membership fee was retained by the Society and the rest was given to the Institute. In 1948, the Society became the International Society for General Semantics (ISGS). *ETC: A Review of General Semantics,* the Society's quarterly journal, was begun in 1943, with S.I. Hayakawa as its editor.

The work of the International Society developed into a greater emphasis on publications, while the Institute concentrated on teaching and training through seminars. In the mid-1940s, the Society used the IGS mailing list of seminar attendees and prospects in its membership and fundraising campaigns. Many Institute trustees also served on the board of the International Society.

The first "popularization" of general semantics, *The Tyranny of Words* by Stuart Chase, was published in 1938. In the 1940s, additional popularizations rolled off the presses, among them S. I. Hayakawa's *Language in Action* (a Book-of-the-Month-Club selection brought out in 1941), Irving J. Lee's *Language Habits in Human Affairs* (1941), and Wendell Johnson's *People in Quandaries* (1946). There were also articles in *Time* and elsewhere about Korzybski and his ideas, and the list of books and reprints sold by the IGS grew apace. Seminars were held in the spacious living room of the Institute building with students staying at nearby hotels.

The staff of the Institute, on average about six people, remained small and there was very little money. In June 1944, Charlotte Schuchardt became office manager and Korzybski's confidential secretary when Pearl Johnecheck took ill.

In the spring of 1946, the building the Institute was renting was sold and the new owners wanted to live in it. This created a major problem for the Institute, as the August 1946 seminar was enrolled and ready to go. Providentially, Institute trustee Robert Redpath, Jr., who knew the headmaster of Indian Mountain School in Lakeville, Connecticut, was able to secure a seminar site in Lakeville. The new venue provided the opportunity for seminar participants to live together in dormitories.

A decision was made to stay temporarily at Lakeville, as the cost of having an office in New York City was not financially feasible. Kendig bought a large old house in Lime Rock, Connecticut and the Institute became her tenant in December 1946.

Marjorie M. Kendig, the Institute's first Education Director, was a highly talented administrator and very devoted worker for the Institute. Her efforts and know-how were crucial in establishing and developing the program of the IGS. The Institute stayed in Lime Rock for more than three decades.

It was a huge challenge for the Institute staff to function in a rural area, ninety miles from New York, five miles from Lakeville, and multiple miles from a metropolis of more than 2,000. Lime Rock was a "ghost town" in 1946, but there were many well-known private schools in the area.

While reorganizing in Connecticut, the Institute faced some additional challenges, to wit, the Society found it needed all its membership dues to be able to continue to function and could no longer contribute any of them to the Institute. The IGS therefore inaugurated its own membership structure to compensate for funds that it would no longer receive from the Society. In 1947, the Institute became incorporated in the State of Connecticut.

The addition of more trustees, many of them from the New York area, was a plus, and in the years 1947-1950 the Institute schedule was full. Moreover, the New York Society for General

Semantics, founded in 1946, was on the rise and other Societies, such as those in Montreal, Los Angeles, San Francisco, Chicago, and Ann Arbor were also forming. In 1948, the third edition of *Science and Sanity* and *Selections from Science and Sanity*, a compendium put together by Guthrie E. Janssen during his one-year fellowship at the Institute, were published. The following year, a Third Congress on General Semantics was held at the University of Denver and Korzybski gave a seminar at Yale and held a colloquium in which a number of prominent Yale professors participated.

In 1949, Francis P. Chisholm, president of the ISGS since 1947, ran for reelection on a platform based on "unifying" or "merging" the IGS with the ISGS. The Institute and four of six members of the ISGS Governing Board supported this plan in principle. The two ISGS Directors who did not support the unification plan were Editor of *ETC,* S.I. Hayakawa, and Associate Editor, Anatol Rapoport. Hayakawa felt so strongly about the matter that he chose to oppose Chisholm as President of the ISGS. Hayakawa believed the strength of the Society came from its different organizational structure and focus as compared to the Institute.

Despite endorsements from the Institute and the leadership of the New York, Los Angeles, and Boston Societies for General Semantics, Chisholm was not able to prevail against his more publicly prominent opponent and talk of combining the two organizations was put on hold. Hayakawa assumed the duties of the presidency of the ISGS in addition to his duties as Editor of *ETC.* A few years later, the International Society moved its office to San Francisco and several local societies became chapters of that organization.

In 1950, Korzybski was preparing a paper to be delivered at a symposium at the University of Texas. He had almost completed that manuscript when, in the early morning of March first, he suddenly died, a few hours after suffering a coronary thrombosis.

Kendig accepted the trustees' appointment as Acting Director and later Director, and the Institute's staff immersed itself in the urgent tasks ahead. Kendig began the publication of the *General Semantics Bulletin* (the Institute's "yearbook") and two issues came out in 1950. That same year the second edition of *Manhood of Humanity* was published and the August seminar, the first without Korzybski, was presented. Dr. J. Samuel Bois delivered the theoretical lectures at this seminar.

Ray Bontrager subsequently became the chief lecturer on theory, with Harry Holtzman adding an important new dimension of art, or "non-verbal abstracting," as he liked to call it. Neurosurgeon Russell Meyers gave talks relating the functioning of the nervous system to general semantics and Charlotte Selver supplied "sensory awareness" workshops. (Charlotte Schuchardt Read, who acquired that last name when she married famed etymologist and lexicographer Allen Walker Read in 1953, later delivered the sensory awareness workshops.) The Institute also unfurled its version of *Group Dynamics*, a newly developed field in experiential human relations.

In 1952, the IGS instituted the annual Alfred Korzybski Memorial Lecture (AKML), a presentation given by a distinguished individual on a topic of interest in the field of general semantics. William Vogt and Ashley Montagu gave the first AKML talk and a long list of distinguished scholars in various fields working in a non-Aristotelian direction have since followed—individuals such as R. Buckminster Fuller, Abraham Maslow, Gregory Bateson, Albert Ellis, Deborah Tannen, and others.

In the 1960s, Kendig's health began to fail and she found it harder to keep up with the demands of the Director's job. She left that position in 1964, although she served as Interim Director from 1971 to 1975 while she was in and out of the hospital. Charlotte Schuchardt Read became Acting Director at various times when needed, traveling from New York City to Connecticut. Professor Elwood Murray also served as Director for two years (September 1967 to September 1969) with his office at the University of Denver.

During the sixties and seventies, Robert Pula, Milton Dawes, James Broadus, Elton Carter, Allen Flagg, Kenneth Johnson, Elwood Murray, Thomas Nelson, and others advanced the Institute's mission through their teaching and writing. Harry Maynard taught GS classes at Cooper Union in New York and Robert Holston and Jane Heyburn brought GS to the business world. Severen Schaeffer conducted seminars in Paris. In this period the Institute held many of its seminars at the University of Denver or at Colorado Academy (an independent, nonsectarian prep school).

Christopher B. Sheldon—the skipper of the 92-foot sailing ship *Albatross,* which sank in a freak storm in 1961, a disaster that inspired the 1996 movie *White Squall*—followed Elwood Murray as Director for about eight months. After that, Charlotte Schuchardt Read served as Director until April 1983, when Robert Pula was appointed for a three-year term.

In 1983, after thirty-seven years in Connecticut, the Institute decided to sell the sizeable house it occupied in Lime Rock. The IGS membership and publication office was moved to Ridgefield, Connecticut where it was overseen by Tom Nelson's AAV Publishing Company. Robert Pula was the Director at the IGS Baltimore office. However, this arrangement proved too costly to continue so all Institute functions were transferred to Baltimore, a municipality far from the center of IGS activities. That latter circumstance created a need to move closer to New York City.

In the mid-1980s, the IGS hired Marjorie Zelner as Executive Secretary and relocated its administrative setup to office space shared with her husband's business in Englewood, New Jersey.

The Institute's 2,500-book library and archives, however, was kept in storage pending a suitable "home." The Institute's President William Exton, Jr., and a small group of trustees, assisted by Marjorie, ran the Englewood operation on a volunteer basis.

In the early 1990s, the IGS initiated a fundraising campaign to secure money to support a suitable site to hold the library and archives. The upshot was the dedication of "The Alfred Korzybski Research and Study Center" in 1994, in the renovated 19th-century carriage house behind the home of Marjorie and Larry Zelner.

In 2000, Marjorie was diagnosed with cancer and resigned as Executive Director. That same year, Jeff Mordkowitz, a former president of the IGS Board of Trustees, was reelected president and appointed Executive Director by the Institute's trustees. The IGS administrative office moved to his home office in Brooklyn, New York.

Marjorie succumbed to her illness in October 2000. The library and archives remained in the Zelner's carriage house until March 2002, when the Board approved moving them to the Dallas-Fort Worth area in Texas.

In September 2003, the IGS Board accepted plans to merge with the International Society for General Semantics; consolidate the operations of both organizations in Fort Worth, Texas; and search for appropriate property to purchase in Fort Worth as a "permanent" home. The ability to buy such a place was made possible by a sizeable bequest from the estates of Allen Walker Read and his wife Charlotte Schuchardt Read. In November, a home was secured in the Fairmount Historic District of Fort Worth.

In January 2004, The International Society for General Semantics and the Institute of General Semantics officially merged, with Steve Stockdale assuming the duties of Executive Director for the "new" Institute of General Semantics. Administrative functions were transitioned from Concord, California (where the ISGS was headquartered) and Brooklyn.

After renovating and remodeling was completed in September 2005, the Institute's offices, library, archives, and seminar facilities were consolidated in Read House. During this time the Institute also published a website that contained many digitized documents for people to view.

In 2007, Stockdale and some Institute trustees proposed having IGS and all its assets subsumed by Texas Christian University (TCU) to save money and associate the IGS with an academic institution. But the majority of trustees thought the Institute could remain viable as a stand-alone organization if it reduced its expenses, so the proposal to be taken over by TCU was declined.

Stockdale resigned his position in 2007 and Lance Strate, a professor of communication and media studies at Fordham University, assumed the duties of Executive Director in 2008. Strate served as the Institute's director for three years during which time he revived IGS publishing and helped the Institute gain a firmer foothold in academia.

In 2011, for budgetary savings and reasons of efficiency, the Institute board voted to suspend the publication of the *General Semantics Bulletin* and retain *ETC: A Review of General Semantics* as the Institute's sole journal. The trustees also voted to sell Read House and relocate the IGS headquarters to Forest Hills, New York where it was managed by IGS President Martin H. Levinson and a small group of Institute trustees on a voluntary basis. Institute materials were quartered in New York City and at Wiley College in Marshall, Texas, and the IGS bookstore was relocated to Grand Valley State University in Allendale, Michigan.

In 2020, Lance Strate became the president of the Institute of General Semantics. Three years later, the IGS headquarters were moved to Park Avenue South in the borough of Manhattan.

Besides its physical presence in the Big Apple, the IGS is active in the virtual world through its *Semantic Reactions* podcast and Facebook, Instagram, and X accounts. The Institute also has a publishing arm, which regularly puts out books and other printed material. And the IGS has formed affiliations with prominent academic and non-profit social science organizations such as the International Communication Association, the National Communication Association, the Media Ecology Association, and the International Bateson Institute.

As we move deeper into the 21st century, the future looks bright for the Institute of General Semantics as it strives to develop and promote the application of GS ideas and principles to bring about clearer thinking, peaceful interaction, and greater sanity in people's lives.[1]

NOTES

Chapter 1. GS Techniques for Clear Thinking

1. For further reading on cognitive bias see Gleb Tsipursky,
    *Never Go with Your Gut: How Pioneering Leaders Make the
    Best Decisions and Avoid Business Disasters* (Newburyport,
    MA: Career Press, 2019); Rolf Dobelli, *The Art of Thinking
    Clearly* (New York: HarperCollins, 2013); Daniel
    Kahneman, *Thinking, Fast and Slow* (New York: Farrar,
    Straus and Giroux, 2013); and Nassim Nicholas Taleb,
    The Black Swan: The Impact of the Highly Improbable (New
    York: Random House, 2007).

Chapter 3. Manhood of Humanity Revisited

1. Alfred Korzybski, *Manhood of Humanity*, 2nd ed. (Lakeville,
    CT: Institute of General Semantics, 1950), 33-34.
2. Ibid., 44-45.
3. Ibid., 208.
4. H.G. Wells, "Civilization at the Breaking Point," *New York
    Times.* May 27, 1915.
5. Korzybski, *Manhood,* lvi-lvii.

Chapter 4. General Semantics and PTSD

1. Charles S. Myers, "A Contribution to the Study of Shell Shock: Being an Account of Three Cases of Loss of Memory, Vision, Smell, and Taste, Admitted into the Duchess of Westminster's War Hospital, Le Toquet," *The Lancet*, 1, no. 4772, (1915): 316-320.

2. David J. Morris, *The Evil Hours: A Biography of Post-Traumatic Stress Disorder* (Boston: Houghton Mifflin Harcourt, 2015), 1.

3. Douglas Kelley, "The Use of General Semantics and Korzybskian Principles as an Extensional Method of Group Psychotherapy in Traumatic Neurosis," in *General Semantics and Psychotherapy*, Isabel Caro and Charlotte Schuchardt Read, eds. (Brooklyn, NY: Institute of General Semantics, 2003), 43.

4. Douglas Kelley, "The Use of General Semantics and Korzybskian Principles as an Extensional Method of Group Psychotherapy in Traumatic Neurosis," *The Journal of Nervous and Mental Diseases*, 114, no. 3 (1951): 189-220.

5. Kelley in *General Semantics and Psychotherapy*, 49.

6. Ibid., 46.

7. Ibid., 51.

8. Ibid., 51.

9. Bruce I. Kodish, *Korzybski: A Biography* (Pasadena, CA: Extensional Publishing, 2011), 528.

10. Alfred Korzybski, "A Veteran's Re-Adjustment and Extensional Methods," *ETC: A Review of General Semantics*, 3, no. 4 (1946): 256.

11. Ibid., 254-264.

12. The positive effects of delayed reaction, which Korzybski conceived of as a "thalamic/cortical pause," in treating stress and phobic symptoms is further described in Rod Gibson, "Post Traumatic Stress Disorder and the Thalamic/Cortical

Pause," *ETC: A Review of General Semantics*, 57, no. 3 (2000): 354-361.

13. Korzybski, 264.

Chapter 5. General Semantics and Constructive Political Discourse

1. Kenneth G. Johnson, *General Semantics: An Outline Survey*, 3rd rev. ed. (Fort Worth, TX: Institute of General Semantics, 2004), 21.
2. Ibid., 21.

Chapter 6. Antisemitism: A GS Case Study

1. Bruce I. Kodish, *Korzybski: A Biography* (Pasadena. CA: Extensional Publishing, 2011), 141-142.
2. Kodish, 112.
3. Brian Porter, *When Nationalism Began to Hate: Imagining Modern Politics in Nineteenth-Century Poland* (New York: Oxford University Press, 2002), 162.
4. Kodish, 144.
5. Kodish, 141.
6. Kodish, 145.
7. Kodish, 146.
8. Kodish, 146.
9. Alfred Korzybski "Foreword to The Essence of Judaism," in *Alfred Korzybski Collected Writings: 1910-1950*, ed. M. Kendig (Englewood, NJ: Institute of General Semantics, 1990), 401-404.
10. Korzybski, 401.
11. Kodish, 396.
12. Kodish, 147.

13. "Antisemitism Globally," ADL, https://www.adl.org/what-we-do/anti-semitism/antisemitism-globally (accessed January 27, 2022).

Chapter 9. Dating America's Response to Alcohol

1. For further reading on alcohol see Susan Cheever, *Drinking in America: Our Social History* (New York: Twelve, 2015); Andrew Barr, *Drink: A Social History of America* (New York: Carroll & Graf, 1999); W.J. Rorabaugh, *The Alcoholic Republic: An American Tradition* (New York: Oxford, 1979); Mark Edward Lender, *Drinking in America. A History* (New York: Free Press, 1987); Daniel Okrent, *The Rise and Fall of Prohibition* (New York: Scribner, 2010); Edward Slingerland, *Drunk. How We Slipped, Danced, and Stumbled Our Way to Civilization* (New York: Little, Brown Spark, 2021); and David M. Fahey and Jon S. Miller (eds.), *Alcohol and Drugs in North America: A Historical Encyclopedia,* rev. ed. (New York: ABC-Clio, 2013).

Chapter 10. Dating Western Poetry

1. Alfred Korzybski, *Science and Sanity: An Introduction to Non-Aristotelian Systems and General Semantics,* 5th ed., (Fort Worth, TX: Institute of General Semantics, 1995), 437.

Chapter 11. Mapping Language and Rhetoric from the Vietnam War

1. Joseph R. Gregory, "Gen. Vo Nguyan Giap, Who Ousted U.S. From Vietnam, Is Dead," Obituary, *New York Times,*

October 4, 2013, https://www.nytimes.com/2013/10/05/world/asia/gen-vo-nguyen-giap-dies.html (accessed May 2, 2018).

2. Dwight D. Eisenhower: "The President's News Conference," April 7, Online by Gerhard Peters and John T. Woolley, *The American Presidency Project*, https://www.presidency.ucsb.edu/documents/the-presidents-news-conference-361 (accessed April 16, 2018).

3. Alan Axelrod, *The Real History of the Vietnam War: A New Look at the Past* (New York: Sterling, 2013), 81.

4. "Inaugural Address of John F. Kennedy," *Yale Law School Avalon Project*, http://avalon.law.yale.edu/20th_century/keednny.asp (accessed April 8, 2018).

5. Tim Weiner, "Robert S. McNamara, Architect of a Futile War, Dies at 93," Obituary, *New York Times*, July 6, 2009, https://www.nytimes.com/2009/07/07/us/07mcnamara.html (accessed May 4, 2018).

6. Earl H. Tilford, Jr., *Crosswinds: The Air Force's Setup in Vietnam* (College Station, TX: Texas A&M University Press, 2009), 63.

7. William Appleman Williams, Thomas McCormick, Lloyd C. Gardner, and Walter LaFeber, (eds.), *America in Vietnam: A Documentary History* (New York: WW Norton, 1989), 239.

8. Lyndon B. Johnson: "Remarks in Memorial Hall, Akron University," October 21, 1964. Online by Gerhard Peters and John T. Woolley, *The American Presidency Project*, https://www.presidency.ucsb.edu/documents/remarks-memorial-hall-akron-university (accessed May 14, 2018).

9. Frank Rich, "Obama at the Precipice," Opinion, *New York Times*, September 26, 2009, https://www.nytimes.com/2009/09/27/opinion/27rich.html (accessed May 1, 2018).

10. Stanley Karnow, "No, He Wouldn't Have Spared Us Vietnam," *Washington Post,* November 20, 1983, https://www.washingtonpost.com/archive/opinions/1983/11/20/no-he-wouldnt-have-spared-us-vietnam/8164ae04-33b6-4463-99c5-9382ceb2a8bb/?utm_term=.dfe5767bd994 accessed May 1, 2018).

11. George W. Ball, *The Past has Another Pattern: Memoirs* (New York: W.W. Norton & Company, 1983), 366.

12. Michael H. Hunt, *Crises in American Foreign Policy* (New Haven, CT: Yale University Press, 1996), 346.

13. Philip Geyelin, "When Reagan Was Being Reagan," *The Washington Post,* April 22, 1984, https://www.washingtonpost.com/archive/opinions/1984/04/22/when-reagan-was-being-reagan/f6b2531c-9348-4761-aaa4-1d086afd1039/?utm_term=.ca03cc00e860 (accessed May 16, 2018).

14. Alfonso A. Narvaez, "Gen. Curtis LeMay, an Architect of Strategic Air Power, Dies at 83," Obituary, *New York Times,* October 2, 1990, https://www.nytimes.com/1990/10/02/obituaries/gen-curtis-lemay-an-architect-of-strategic-air-power-dies-at-83.html (accessed April 21, 2018).

15. Albin Krebs, "George Aiken, Longtime Senator and G.O.P. Maverick, Dies at 92," Obituary, *New York Times,* November 20, 1984, https://www.nytimes.com/1984/11/20/obituaries/george-aiken-longtime-senator-and-gop-maverick-dies-at-92.html (accessed April 8, 2018).

16. William James Stover and Diane Elizabeth Dreher, "Paradigms of Conflict: The Language of the Vietnam War," *Peace Research* 20 no. 2 (May 1988): 44.

17. Memo by Robert S. McNamara to President Johnson, October 14, 1966, in *The Pentagon Papers, New York Times* (New York: Bantam Books, 1971), 549.

18. Geoffrey Perret, *Commander in Chief: How Truman, Johnson, and Bush Turned a Presidential Power into a Threat to America's Future* (New York: Farrar, Straus and Giroux, 2008), 277.

19. R.W. Apple Jr., "McNamara Recalls, and Regrets, Vietnam," *New York Times,* April 9. 1995, https://www.nytimes.com/1995/04/09/world/mcnamara-recalls-and-regrets-vietnam.html (accessed May 14, 2018).

20. James M. Lindsay, "The Vietnam War in Forty Quotes," *The Waters Edge,* Council on Foreign Relations, April 30, 2015, https://www.cfr.org/blog/vietnam-war-forty-quotes (accessed April 8, 2018).

21. James Pringle, "Meanwhile: The quiet town where the Vietnam War began," Opinion, *New York Times,* March 23, 2004, https://www.nytimes.com/2004/03/23/opinion/meanwhile-the-quiet-town-where-the-vietnam-war-began.html (accessed April8, 2018).

22. Guy Raz, "Final Words: Cronkite's Vietnam Commentary," All Things Considered, *NPR,* June 18, 2009, https://www.npr.org/templates/story/story.php?storyId=106775685 (accessed April 8, 2018).

23. Susan Ratcliffe, ed., *Oxford Essential Quotations*, 4th ed., online version, 2016, "Vietnam War," Oxford University Press, http://www.oxfordreference.com/view/10.1093/acref/9780191826719.001.0001/q-oro-ed4-00011177 (accessed April 8, 2018).

24. David F. Schmitz, "Congress Must Draw the Line," in *Vietnam and the American Political Tradition: The Politics of Dissent*, edited by Randall Woods (New York: Cambridge University Press, 2003), 140.

25. David Remnick, "Nattering Nabobs," *The New Yorker,* July 10, 2006, https://www.newyorker.com/magazine/2006/07/10/nattering-nabobs (accessed April 21, 2018).

26. Benjamin Hedin, "Martin Luther King's Searing Anti-War Speech Fifty Years Later," *The New Yorker,* April 3, 2017, https://www.newyorker.com/culture/culture-desk/martin-luther-king-jr-s-searing-antiwar-speech-fifty-years-later (accessed April 16, 2018).

27. Bob Orkand, "'I Ain't Got No Quarrel With Them Vietcong,'" Opinion, *New York Times,* March 23, 2004, https://www.nytimes.com/2017/06/27/opinion/muhammad-ali-vietnam-war.html (accessed April 16, 2018).

28. David F. Schmitz, *The Tet Offensive: Politics, War, and Public Opinion* (New York: Rowan & Littlefield, 2005), 145.

29. Rick Perlstein, *Nixonland: The Rise of a President and the Fracturing of America* (New York: Scribner; Reprint edition, 2010), 249.

30. Robert Mitchell, "A 'Pearl Harbor in politics'; LBJ's stunning decision not to seek re-election," Retropolis, *Washington Post,* March 31, 2018, https://www.washingtonpost.com/news/retropolis/wp/2018/03/31/a-pearl-harbor-in-politics-lbjs-stunning-decision-not-to-seek-reelection/?utm_term=.f2279eb338a8 (accessed April 21, 2018).

31. Tom Wicker, *JFK and LBJ: The Influence of Personality on Politics* (New York: William Morrow, 1968), 278.

32. Alan Axelrod, *The Real History of the Vietnam War* (New York: Sterling, 2013), 268.

33. James G. Zumwalt, *Bare Feet, Iron Will: Stories from the Other Side of Vietnam's Battlefields* (Jacksonville, FL: Fortis Publishing, 2010), 334.

34. Peter Baker, "Nixon Tried to Spoil Johnson's Vietnam Peace Talks in '68, Notes Show," *New York Times,* January 2, 2017, https://www.nytimes.com/2017/01/02/us/politics/nixon-tried-to-spoil-johnsons-vietnam-peace-talks-in-68-notes-show.html (accessed May 25, 2018).

35. Richard Nixon: "Address to the Nation on the War in Vietnam," November 3, 1969, Online by Gerhard Peters and John T. Woolley, *The American Presidency Project*, https://www.presidency.ucsb.edu/documents/address-the-nation-the-war-vietnam (accessed April 8, 2018).

36. Timothy Maga, *The 1960s* (New York: Facts on File, 2003), 268.

37. Alexander DeConde, "Presidential Power—Presidential war in Vietnam," *Encyclopedia of the New American Nation*, http://www.americanforeignrelations.com/O-W/Presidential-Power-Presidential-war-in-vietnam.html (accessed April 8, 2018).

38. Haldeman, H.R., *The Ends of Power* (New York: Times Books, 1978), 122.

39. "Melvin Laird: Richard Nixon Administration," *Historical Office of the Secretary of Defense*, http://history.defense.gov/Multimedia/Biographies/Article-View/Article/571291/melvin-r-laird/ (accessed April 8, 2018).

40. Daniel Ellsberg, "Daniel Ellsberg: Himself (former aide Defense Dept., RAND Corp.)," *IMDb*, https://www.imdb.com/title/tt0071604/characters/nm0255281 (accessed May 18, 2018).

41. "Transcript: Kerry Testifies Before Senate Panel 1971," *NPR*, April 25, 2006, https://www.npr.org/templates/story/story.php?storyId=3875422 (accessed May 25, 2018).

42. Jak Phillips, "Nobel-Winner Wrangling: Henry Kissinger," *Time*, October 7, 2011, http://content.time.com/time/specials/packages/article/0,28804,2096389_2096388_2096386,00.html (accessed April 29, 2018).

43. Gerald R. Ford: "Address at a Tulane University Convocation," April 23, 1975. Online by Gerhard Peters and John T.

Woolley, *The American Presidency Project*, https://www. presidency.ucsb.edu/documents/address-tulane-university-convocation (accessed April 8, 2018).

44. Ronald Reagan, "Address to the Veterans of Foreign Wars Convention in Chicago," August 18, 1980. Online by Gerhard Peters and John T. Woolley, *The American Presidency Project*, https://www.presidency.ucsb.edu/documents/address-the-veterans-foreign-wars-convention-chicago (accessed April 8, 2018).

45. Lloyd C. Gardner and Marilyn B. Young, *Iraq and the Lessons of Vietnam, Or, How Not to Learn from the Past* (New York: New Press, 2008), 9.

46. Ronald H. Spector, "Vietnam War," *Encyclopedia Britannica*, https://www.britannica.com/event/Vietnam-War (accessed May 4, 2018).

Chapter 12. What the Fuck: Examining an "Obscene" Term

1. Allen Walker Read, "An Obscenity Symbol," *American Speech* 9, no. 4 (1934): 264-78.

2. Scholars have dated two instances of "fuck" that appeared in print before 1528, but because one is Scottish and the other appears in code, with a Latin verb conjugation, they are often not given the credit for first use.

3. "Starr Report," *New York Times,* September 12, 1998.

4. Ruth Wajnryb, *Expletive Deleted: A Good Look at Bad Language* (New York: Free Press, 2011), 40.

5. Richard Dooling, *Blue Streak: Swearing, Free Speech, and Sexual Harassment* (New York: Random House, 1996), 18.

6. Read, "An Obscenity Symbol," 264.

7. John McWhorter, *Nine Nasty Words: English in the Gutter: Now, Then, and Forever* (New York: Avery, 2021), 43.
8. Ibid, 5.

Chapter 13. Indexing the American Revolutionary War

1. For further reading on the revolutionary war see Gordon S. Wood, *The American Revolution: A History* (New York: Modern Library, 2003); Edmund S. Morgan, *The Birth of the Republic, 1763-1789*, 4th ed. (Chicago: University of Chicago Press, 2012); Alan Taylor, *American Revolutions: A Continental History, 1750-1804* (New York: Norton, 2016); Nick Bunker, *An Empire on the Edge: How Britain Came to Fight America* (New York: Vintage, 2015); John Ferling, *Almost a Miracle: The American Victory in the War of Independence* (New York: Oxford, 2009); and David K. Allison and Larrie D. Ferreiro, eds., *The American Revolution: A World War* (Washington, DC: Smithsonian Books, 2018).

Coda. A Brief History of the Institute of General Semantics

1. For additional information on the history of the Institute of General Semantics see Bruce I. Kodish, *Korzybski: A Biography* (Pasadena, CA: Extensional Publishing, 2011), 438-623; Charlotte Schuchardt Read, "The Institute of General Semantics: A Brief Historical Survey" *General Semantics Bulletin* 54 (1988-1989): 62-68; Steve Stockdale, "Snooping Around the Time-Binding Attic" *ETC: A Review of General Semantics* 59, no. 1 (Spring 2002): 90-99;

"The Institute and the Society: A Self-Reflexive Assessment of Two Organizations, One Discipline, and General Semantics" *ETC: A Review of General Semantics* 60, no. 3 (Fall 2003): 271-280.

Index

presidential elections, disunity over, 79–84, 87–89
presidential misconduct, disunity over, 89–90
presidential term limits, 86
probability thinking, 31–32
"The Profiteers and How to Fight Them" (Korzybski), 62–63
Prohibition Era, 97–99
Prohibition Party, 96–97
Protocols of the Elders of Zion, 64–66
PTSD (posttraumatic stress disorder), 45–51
Pula, Robert, 171
Puritans, 92

Raleigh, Sir Walter, 107
Ramsour's Mill, Battle of, 142
Rapoport, Anatol, 169
Read, Allen Walker, 138–39, 170, 172
"An Obscenity Symbol," 133
Read, Charlotte Schuchardt, 167, 170–72
Reagan, Ronald, 123, 131
Reconstruction, 72, 84–85
Redpath, Robert, Jr., 168
refrigerators in the home, 99
religious biases, 74–75
Republicans vs. Democrats, 78, 83–84, 86–90
Reverdy, Pierre: *Departure*, 114
Revere, Paul, 93
Revolutionary War, 79, 93, 140–48
Rich, Adrienne, 109
rifles, 41–42
Rilke, Rainer Maria, 109
Rimbaud, Arthur: *Memory*, 109
Der Ring des Nibelungen (Wagner), 106–7
Roback, A.A., 67–68
Roe v. Wade, 74
Roosevelt, Franklin, 85–86, 99

Rostow, Walt W., 124
rum, 92–93, 100, 144
Rush, Benjamin: "An Enquiry into the Effects of Spirituous Liquors," 94
Russian Revolution, 64

Salinger, J.D.: *Catcher in the Rye*, 135
Sappho, 103–4
sarcasm, 55
Saunders, James A., 48–49
Schaeffer, Severen, 171
Science and Sanity (Korzybski), 37, 39, 48, 102, 164–66, 169
scientific method, 23, 37–38, 50
SDS (Students for a Democratic Society), 126
Second American Congress on General Semantics, 166
The Second Coming (Yeats), 111
Second Indochina War, 118–19
self-righteousness, 55
Selver, Charlotte, 170
"Semantic Antics" (satire), 156–58
Semantic Reactions, 174
semantics, defined, 19
separate-but-equal policy, 71–72
Seven Years War, 147
Sexton, Anne, 113
Shakespeare, William, 105, 107
sharecroppers, 84–85
Shave 'Em Dry (Brogan), 136
Sheldon, Christopher B., 171
Shelley, Percy Bysshe, 109
shell shock (*now* PTSD), 45–51
signal reactions, 21
Six Sermons on Intemperance (Beecher), 93
Skynner, Robin, 166
slavery, 71, 83–84, 145–46
Smith, Bob, 100
snipers, 42
Social Credit, 65